尋訪失落的香格里拉

尋訪失落的香格里拉

序 ཀ་ཆེ་པ་ཙན་དང་།

金·羅絲貝莉(Kim Roseberry)
是個癡迷的香格里拉信徒。她不
是只從書面或字眼去感知這個奇
幻的地名,而這個世界絕大多數
人都還只停留在這個層面上。

香格里拉在西藏有另一個名字,香巴拉。由於多年生活在西藏的
緣故,我個人更認同這個香巴拉。有一首旋律美極了的民歌:「有一個美麗
的地方/人們都把它嚮往/那裡四季常青/那裡鳥語花香/它的名字叫香巴拉/傳
說是神仙居住的地方。」香巴拉確乎是藏族心裡的天堂。

羅絲貝莉10歲的時候,第一次從她爸爸那裡知道了香格里拉,開始了她
最初的關於這個奇幻之地的想像。18歲時的羅絲貝莉曾經有過一個她自己的
香格里拉,是她家鄉一處樹林中屬於她個人的秘地,那裡藏著她的寧靜與玄
思,藏著一個少女的天堂之夢。她的香格里拉之旅從家鄉的樹林中起航的。

第一個真切的香格里拉對年輕的羅絲貝莉來得太快太突然了。那是她第
一次到北京,她住進了香格里拉酒店。對她而言,曾經激發出無限想像的東
方名字具體為「富麗堂皇的大門,水晶般閃閃發光的枝形吊燈……覆蓋著上
好白色亞麻布的活動小桌送來了裝在銀器裡的早餐」。而當時她只有19歲。是
她的幸運還是她的悲哀呢?

2000年她22歲。她來到中國雲南一個叫中甸的小城。給她的印象是大地
的木材、石塊、泥土搭建的房屋,她想像它們是從大地中生長出來的,想像

它們最終回歸大地。她還記住了不和諧的鋼筋水泥建築物和更不和諧的漫天飛舞的白色塑膠袋。中甸的記憶中最有價值的是幾乎不流逝的時間和從容不迫的生活。

當時她沒有想過（絕對想不到），這裡在一年之後將更名為令她魂牽夢縈的香格里拉。

這裡就是香格里拉。

這裡就是香格里拉！

這裡就是香格里拉？

中甸於是成了羅絲貝莉一來再來的地方。她當然喜歡這裡；豈止是喜歡，說迷戀也不為過。但她的香格里拉夢已經開始透光，夢似乎不再是夢。一個具體的夢之地本身就是一個悖論。因虛無而美妙的夢想被具體被定格，就像為混沌開出七竅一樣，想像突然走到了盡頭。「神話消失了，按照自己的觀念來定義香格里拉的那種自由永遠消失了。」

中甸的再命名生出了令人目眩的光環，真如雨後霓虹一般絢麗，也如霓虹一般短命。今天的香格里拉與周莊、曲阜、亞龍灣一般無二，都只是中國旅遊地圖上的一處景點，如此而已。幻覺不再。但是羅絲貝莉還是愛上了美麗的雲南，她把這裡當做青春的駐腳地，她在這裡住下來，往返於德欽、中甸、梅里雪山之間的壯觀。她拍了很多照片，結識了更多的藏族朋友，她逐漸把自己融入到那片偉美的山川之中。

我沒見過羅絲貝莉，我更願意想像她是個美麗的女孩，因為這些充滿靈性的文字，也因為她充滿虔誠的香巴拉夢想。

馬原 於北京

目錄

人人都在尋找香格里拉

　　香格里拉，一個最近在亞洲和其他地方備受關注的名字。這個名字隱藏著一片遙遠神秘的大地，使人產生無限遐想：覆蓋著銀色冰雪的巍峨群山下，披著棕色袈裟的僧侶舉行著古老神秘的儀式，將人帶回詹姆斯·希爾頓（James Hilton）在1933年寫的《消失的地平線》中所描繪的情景。今天，好像人人都在尋找香格里拉。許多亞洲國家都聲稱「真正」的香格里拉在他們那裡，一些賓館、旅遊點和旅行社都利用這個名字推出了類似世外桃源的地方來掩飾他們真正的商業動機。這個名字吸引了成群結隊的旅遊者來到了過去不為人知的地方，現在這個名字甚至也出現在酒和香煙的廣告上。

　　Shangri-la, it is a name that has recently garnered much attention in Asia and around the world. The word is shrouded in the mystery of faraway, exotic lands and brings to mind images of sharp mountain peaks draped in thick layers of silken snow, under which maroon-clad monks perform esoteric rituals that hark back to a time period as far away as the imaginary land popularized in James Hilton's 1933 book Lost Horizon. Today, it seems that everyone is searching for Shangri-la. Numerous Asian countries claim to hold the "real" Shangri-la within their borders, and hotels, resorts and travel agencies are snatching up the name to promote the paradisiacal escape that they all hope to sell. The name attracts droves of tourists to previously unknown areas and now adorns the labels of even cigarettes and alcohol.

中甸

　　我目前生活在中國西南的雲南省，這個國家的官方聲稱這裡是香格里拉的故鄉。我所到之處，「香格里拉」這個詞充斥在看板、電視螢幕和報紙上。在大街上、商店和飯館裡，人們嘴裡也常常叨念著這個詞。這個似乎無處不在的總被提及的詞有著夢幻般的特性。每一個人對香格里拉都有一個想像和概念，即使他們從來沒有去過擁有這個名字的地方。圍繞著這個世外桃源的種種說法，我自然也產生了自己的一些想法，雖然我第一次產生「香格里拉」這個朦朧的觀念是在來中國之前。然後我來到雲南，見識了以「香格里拉」命名的這片土地，當我坐在這兒撰寫這個稿件時，慢慢形成了對香格里拉的看法。也許這只是我自己尋找香格里拉的經過。

藏族村落

I currently live in China's southwestern province of Yunnan, home to the country's official Shangri-la. Everywhere I turn, I see the word splashed out on billboards, across the television screen, in the newspapers. I hear it from the mouths of people walking down the street, in the shops and restaurants. There is a dreamlike quality that surrounds this word and people tune in whenever "Shangri-la" is mentioned. Everyone appears to have an image and idea of what Shangri-la is, even if they have never visited any place by the name. Being so surrounded by the stir regarding this earthly paradise, I naturally have some ideas of my own, though my first encounter with the concept of Shangri-la came well before my travels to China. Since first coming to Yunnan, to the first time I visited the area known as Shangri-la, to today, as I sit here writing this script, my vision of this earthly paradise has continued to develop and transform. This is a chronicle of my relationship to, and perhaps my own search for, the dream of Shangri-la.

藏族婦女

香格里拉：我的避難所

　　1988年12月，緬因州。那時我還只是一個10歲的小女孩。一天下午3點，校車到了我家農場，我拎著書包下了車，穿過雪地回家。我清楚地聽到一些同學叫喊著：「啊！好臭啊！」由於害羞，那時我不敢說出所有的不滿。我脫下不合身的堂姐的舊校服，換上散發著牛糞味的工作服到牛棚清掃牛糞，然後用手推車拉來鋸末渣子撒在地上，還要給饑餓的牛餵草，牠們的鼻子在陰冷的空氣中冒著熱氣。我去找爸爸，他正在牛奶房擠牛奶。從清晨6點一直到晚上7點半，他都要在這裡做事。我告訴他，我想去騎馬。「幹什麼，你想去找香格里拉？」爸爸沒好氣地問。那時我完全不明白這個詞的意思，猜測著好像是一個世外桃源，我點頭。套上我的小馬，揚鞭穿過農場的原野向密林深處飛奔，那是我的避難所。

緬因州　農場上的牛

　　1988. December. Maine. I am ten years old. Three in the afternoon. I step off the school bus carrying my middle school books and walk across the snow to my house. I can still hear the other children's cries as they shout "Eww! It stinks!" I didn't say anything; I never did. I am so shy that I hardly speak at all. I change out of my school clothes, hand-me-downs from my older cousins that never really fit well, into my barn clothes that smell of the cows outside. In the barn, I pick up a hoe and begin scraping out the many cow stalls. Clean, I grab the sawdust cart, fill it, and begin wheeling it down the aisle, spreading the sawdust in layers underneath the cows. I push a wheelbarrow filled with grain and dole out a portion to each cow. Lastly, I break open hay bales and toss leaves in front of the hungry mouths breathing puffs of moisture into the cool air. Finished, I go to see my father who is in the milk room milking the cows. He has been there since six that morning and will not be finished until half past seven that night. I tell him I am going for a horseback ride. "Off to find Shangri-la, are you?" he asks. I don't really know what the word means, but I figure it is some sort of paradise, and so I nod and go back into the barn, grab my pony's bridle off its nail, and after fitting the bit into his mouth, swing myself up onto my pony's broad back. Out we gallop, across the vast fields towards the patch of woods that are my sanctuary.

頭髮在風中飛舞，馬蹄撞擊地面的聲音使我激盪，我感覺到將我帶離農場奔向遠方的力量和速度。同學的羞辱使我臉上火辣辣的，感覺不到撲面的寒風。在農場生活是一種恥辱。穿著塑膠鞋是一種恥辱。身著舊衣服是一種恥辱。爸爸到學校來穿著做事的衣服和橡膠鞋，渾身上下都帶著牛棚的污垢和氣味是一種恥辱。我希望我能成爲其他的人，到其他的地方去。我牽著馬漫無目的地在樹林中溜達，然後爬到樹上坐著，看著眼前冰雪覆蓋的大地，想像著香格里拉應該是個什麼樣美好的地方。我敢打賭，香格里拉的空氣一定比花朵還要溫暖甜蜜，而且陽光燦爛，到處都是棕櫚樹。我想像我在那裡一定穿著眞正的皮鞋，也絕對沒有討厭的牛。隨風搖動的樹枝的沙沙聲使我平靜下來，我在逃避現實的想像中升騰，穿過樹林和大地來到雲端深處，那裡，美妙的天堂正等待著我。

　　The wind blows through my hair, the sound of my pony's hooves pounding the earth bounces up at me, and I can feel the power and speed of the animal below me that is carrying me away from the farm. The wind cannot cool the burn of my face as I think of my classmate's taunts. I am ashamed of living on a farm. I am ashamed that my shoes are made of vinyl and not of leather. I am ashamed that my clothes are all second-hand. I am ashamed of my father when he comes into the school dressed in his farm overalls and rubber boots that carry the dirt and smell of the barn. I wish I could be someone else, somewhere else. I get off my horse and walk into the woods. I climb up a tree and sit there, looking at the snow-covered ground below me. I think of what Shangri-la must be like. I bet the air is warm and sweeter than flowers, that palm trees grow everywhere and the sun always shines. I picture myself there and see that I am wearing leather shoes and cows do not exist. The rustle of the branches above me lulls me and I escape upwards, passing through the trees, above the fields into the clouds where paradise waits for me.

緬因州　通向樹林的路。我曾在上面騎馬馳騁，將我引向秘密的「香格里拉」

緬因州　初冬

▼ 失落的夢中天堂

　　1996年9月，緬因州。明天，我要離開家鄉去上大學。我把所有的東西塞進行李箱，爭取一些時間在農場走一走，和它、和我的童年說再見。突然，我想起了我在樹林裡的秘密據點，爸爸把它叫做我的「香格里拉」。我有許多年沒去那裡了，急於離開這個地方帶來了一些辛酸的回憶。我走出家門，踏著修剪過的綠色草坪，邁著堅定的步子朝樹林走去。我經過原野中一株孤獨的榆樹，樹下有兩匹馬在安詳地吃草。樹林邊緣有一片空地，突然，我的腦海中出現了以前夢中天堂的畫面：一條晶瑩清澈的溪水涓涓注入一個小小的池塘，周圍覆蓋著厚厚苔蘚的岩石。我走進樹林，本能引導著我向童年的舞臺走去，那裡曾經上演了我無數的幻想。

Kim Roseberry 李玉祥／攝

1996. September. Maine. Tomorrow, I leave home for college. I have packed all my things into suitcases and boxes and am taking this time to walk about the farm and say my goodbyes to this place and my child-hood days. I suddenly remember my secret spot in the woods that my dad called my "Little Shangri-la". I haven't been there in many years, but the anticipation and anxiety of leaving have brought back memory with certain pungency. I set off from the house and strike out across the files of long, green grass towards the woods. I pass by the lone elm tree in the field, under which two horses graze contentedly. There is a break in the edge of the woods and, suddenly, in my mind I can see my former piece of paradise - a small pool fed by a trickling rivulet of crystal-clear water surrounded by rocks covered in thick green moss. I enter the woods and let my instincts guide me towards the place that was stage for so many of my childhood fantasies.

緬因州　農場上的小屋

我走在樹林裡，眼睛盯著潮濕樹葉覆蓋的土地，搜尋著我以前避難所的蛛絲馬跡。走啊、走啊，感覺像在繞圈子，圍著樹林走了很多圈，但都不能找到與夢中仙境相似的地方。除了踩在柔軟土地上的樹葉發出的沙沙聲，四周一片寂靜。它就在小山的後面嗎？不。也許在那兒，在那株老橡樹的後面。不，不在那裡。在那兒嗎？不。在這兒？不，不，不。我找不到我的小池塘了。它已經消失了，或許我再也找不到了。或許我已太久沒有來過這裡。也許我現在的生活已發生了非常大的變化，又或許是我自己改變了許多。或許，我的香格里拉在別處。

碧塔海 樹林

I walk among the trees, my eyes plying the damp, leaf-covered ground, searching for a sign of my former escape. I walk and walk, seemingly in circles, and yet cannot spot anything resembling the image in my mind. There is silence, aside from the sound of my steps as they rustle wet leaves on the soft ground. Could it be there, just behind that little knoll? No. Maybe there, behind that old oak tree. No. Over there? No. There? No. No. No. I cannot find my little pool. It has disappeared and maybe I will never find it again. Maybe it has been too long since I visited. Maybe my life is too different now, or maybe I have changed too much. Maybe my Shangri-la lies elsewhere.

大學，另一個世界

　　1996年12月，大學。在這個新地方我沒什麼自信。這所明星大學與我成長的地方有天壤之別。我的同學都是一些有錢人。他們來自國內最好的學校，對於未來進入上流社會充滿信心。禮堂那頭的男孩有著屬於自己的飛機，圖書館是以其祖父的名字命名的。我同學的父母都是醫生、律師或有名的政治家，像我爸爸這樣的人永遠跟他們沒有關聯。我以前從來沒有聽到有人用這樣的方式交談，他們使用的辭彙只出現在字典裡。在這些人面前我覺得自己十分渺小。我嫉妒他們，嚮往著有一天能過像他們那樣富裕的生活。

緬因州　初冬　農場的路

　　1996. December. College. I am not sure of myself in this new place. This ivy-league college is a separate world from where I grew up. My classmates are of the truly rich. They come from the finest prep schools in the country and walk with the confidence that their futures are already assured among the upper crust of high society. The boy down the hall has his own plane and the library is named after his grandfather. My classmate's parents are doctors, lawyers, and famous politicians - people with whom my father could never find a topic to speak about. I have never heard people talk the way these people talk, using words that I have to look up in the dictionary. I feel so small next to these people. I look at them with a touch of envy, and long to taste a day in the life of the rich.

香格里拉，
一定是天堂

在前往江蘇的火車上　李玉祥／攝

北京，香格里拉飯店

　　1997年6月，北京。計程車載著我穿過夜幕下的街道。這是我第一次來中國。車輛穿越夜晚的喧嘩；點著露天燈泡的夜市人潮湧動；建築工地的強光照射著嘈雜的黑暗，這裡同時進行著毀滅和創造；穆斯林男子站在天橋的陰影裡，用扇子對烤羊肉串的煤爐搧風；夜總會的霓虹燈瘋狂閃爍。路上擠滿了公車、轎車和自行車，它們在此起彼落的噪音裡緩緩移動。在這樣的混亂中卻有著某種我熟悉的東西。在這一片喧鬧之上，我看到由巨大、閃爍螢光的字母組成的「香格里拉」。招牌下是一家五星級的豪華酒店。「香格里拉」聽起來如同滾滾而來的金子。我覺得自己似乎正通過一扇富麗堂皇的大門，水晶般閃閃發光的吊燈下是柔軟的地毯。一位戴著白手套的年輕男人接過我的行李，引導我來到電梯旁，電梯送我到房間，那裡，即便是深秋，也還是有新鮮的水果在等著我。每一件東西都是閃閃發光的。柔軟的床和乾淨舒適的被褥。我也不必在清晨整理房間，陌生的女服務生會來打掃。覆蓋著質料好的白色亞麻布的活動小桌送來盛裝在銀器裡的早餐。用餐時，微微閃光的銀器發出的柔和叮噹聲就好像是在輕輕敲打著精緻的瓷器。所有的一切，對我來說都是奢侈的，似乎表明只有重要的人物才能享受。香格里拉一定是天堂。

　　1997. June. Beijing. A taxi takes me through the night streets. This is my first visit to China. The car passes through the chaos of the late hours; night markets lit by bare light bulbs to which people flock; floodlights on construction zones where simultaneous destruction and creation light the darkness with noise; Muslim men with fans standing in the shadows of overpasses beating wind over the coals that roast kebabs; flashing neon lights of night clubs. The lanes are crowded by buses, cars and bicycles all moving in un-orchestrated rhythm. It is a chaos that holds a certain familiarity for me.

Shangri-la. I see the word rising out of the chaos, written in bold fluorescent letters. Underneath it lays a luxurious hotel with five stars to its name. The word sounds like dripping gold. I wonder what it would be like to walk through the shining doors, over the plush carpet underneath the glittering crystal chandelier. I wonder how it would feel to have a young man wearing white gloves reach for my bags and point the way to an elevator that would lead me up many floors to a room where, even though it was fall, fresh fruit lay waiting for me. Everything would glitter. The bed would be soft and the sheets cool and crisp. In the morning I wouldn't have to worry about making the bed; an unseen maid would straighten up after me. My breakfast would be taken at a table covered in fine white linen and set with silverware that would gleam and make soft clinking sounds as it struck the fine porcelain. I wonder what it would feel like to experience such luxury. I wonder what it would be like to feel so important. This Shangri-la must be paradise.

納西村

正在晾曬的向日葵花盤和玉米

印度，酒店什麼也沒有

　　1997年9月，印度。我待在一家五星級酒店裡。房間乾淨得連空氣中都散發著消毒水的氣味。床和沙發也很舒適。電視有許多頻道，晚上會播放電影。但是在印度，當外面充滿了色彩、生活氣息和有趣的文化時，誰還會想待在房間裡看美國的電視節目？酒店的食物很棒，但外面小飯館的食物更好且便宜。服務生隨叫隨到，他們尊稱我爲「女士」，但其他客人以好笑的目光看著我，似乎我並不屬於這裡。住在這裡很好，舒適惬意，不過僅此而已。除此之外，酒店什麼也沒有，我覺得有點失望。

　　1997. September. India. I stay in a five-star hotel. The room is nice, but the air smells sterile. The bed is comfortable, as is the sofa. The television has lots of channels and at night, they play movies, but who wants to stay inside and watch American TV programs when they are in India and the outside is full of colour, life and interesting culture? The food is good, but not that much better than what I paid a fraction of the cost for at a small restaurant outside. The staff is exceedingly helpful, and they all call me "madam", but other guests give me funny looks, as if I do not belong here. I had a good, comfortable stay, but that was it. The hotel offered nothing more than that and I felt a little disappointed.

在藏族的婚禮上

巨變必將來到這個地方

　　2000年10月，中旬。我外出爬山。風在我耳邊呼嘯並刮得我的臉生痛。我的頭頂上方是五顏六色的經幡，有紅、黃、白、綠和藍色，它們被拴在長長的繩子上，呈拱架狀橫過天空。經幡被風吹得劈啪作響，好像是要將寫在上面的祈禱帶給佛主。一座小山的山頂聳立著一座小小的白色佛塔，煙霧順著塔頂的洞口盤旋繚繞。我的鼻子裡充滿了這種神聖的味道。舉目四望，山下世俗的城市在擴展蔓延。沿著石頭鋪就的小路，我從佛主的聖地到山下的公路，向城市走去。當我穿越一片荒地時，一陣狂風掠過荒原，我只好轉身背對刺人的沙塵。排水溝散發著惡臭，棕色的土地橫七豎八地立著柵欄，柵欄上尖利的帶刺鐵絲掛著數以千計的「小旗」，它們也在風中劈啪作響。這些「小旗」就像山上的經幡一樣繽紛多彩。雖然上面沒有文字，但卻以同樣的劈啪作響來抗議人類的粗心大意。這是被當作廢物丟棄的塑膠袋，四處飛散。

中甸　田野中的神祠。裊裊的香煙正在升起

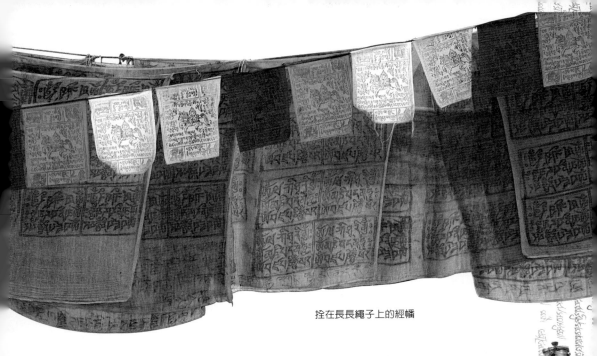

拴在長長繩子上的經幡

2000. October. Zhongdian. I walk up the mountain. The wind thunders in my ears and bites my face. Above me, prayer flags in red, yellow, white, green and blue are strung across the sky in long, arching lines. The wind makes the flags snap and carries the prayers written on them to the gods. At the top of the small mountain stands a small white stupa, smoke curling from the hole in the side. The holy smell of incense fills my nostrils. I look down from the mountain to the valley where man's city spreads itself out. Descending from the place of the gods down the stony path to the level land, I turn towards the city. As I walk across the barren land, dust clouds hurl themselves at me and I turn my back against the sting. From the gutter, I smell the stench of man. Cutting across the brown earth are fences and from them comes the rustle of hundreds, maybe thousands, of flags strung across the sharp barbed wire. These flags, like the flags on the mountain, are also of many colours, but have no prayers written on them. Yet, they speak loudly of man's carelessness. They are plastic bags that have been cast aside as trash and have blown across the land to be caught in this fence.

這是我第一次到中甸，那時它還沒有獲得「世外桃源——香格里拉」的美譽。我在那兒只待了幾天，印象最深的是被風吹得鼓脹的塑膠袋，它們在空氣中迴旋，隨著陣陣寒風在土地上飄蕩。它們無處不在，這種無法逃避的景觀讓我相當沮喪。我覺得悲哀，這種現代社會的廢棄物居然侵入了一個聖潔的藏族小城。

在中甸，隨處可以看到人與自然之間的融洽和衝突。在城郊，藏族人在貧瘠的土地上耕作只是索取基本的生存。當我透過照相機的鏡頭觀看那些傳統房屋時，我看到它們和周圍的景色融為一體，這些房屋的材料來自於大地的泥土、石塊和木材，使得它們好像是從大地中生長出來一樣，最終也會回歸大自然。在這些屋子裡，四季的循環往復、生與死、創造與瓦解，不動聲色地持續進行著。

This was my first trip to Zhongdian, before it acquired the status of paradise. I only spent a few days there, but the lasting image in my mind was of puffy plastic bags, floating and swirling through the air, riding on the sharp gusts of wind that blew across the land. They were everywhere and I was dismayed at the inescapable sight. It saddened me to see this invasion of modern wastefulness upon this little Tibetan city. In Zhongdian, the relationships of harmony and discord between man and the earth were so apparent as I moved through the city and out into the surrounding plains. On the outskirts of the city, the Tibetans work the harsh soil by hand and draw their existence from it. As I took in the traditional architecture there with my camera lens, I saw no disruption of the scenery, for homes are built from the earth - of mud, stone and wood. They are a seemingly inseparable part and continuation of the land. Eventually, these buildings will return to the earth from which they come. In these buildings, the natural cycles of seasons, life and death, creation and disintegration are exhibited in a smooth, continuous rhythm.

公路上方的藏族村落

松贊林寺中的神像

然而，鋼筋水泥的建築破壞了這樣的和諧美麗。它們無法與大地融爲一體，而是高高地、孤獨地聳立著，以這種方式來彰顯它們的存在。隨著時光流逝，我想鋼筋水泥的世界會像塑膠袋一樣肆意擴張，侵蝕土地、人類和文化。自從這裡改名爲「香格里拉」以來，我很開心看到這裡已經禁止隨意丟棄塑膠袋，城市和土地比過去乾淨多了。中國和國外的相關機構對這片地區的關注帶來了許多積極的變化，有助於保護中國這片獨特而又遼闊的自然景色。但是現代化是必然的發展，這將迫使這裡一直存在的傳統生活成爲過去，迫使居民和土地分離。巨變必將來到這個小地方。如果10年後我再來到這裡，供奉佛主的香煙和經幡是否還會在現代化的城市上空飄蕩？

Concrete and steel buildings create a disruption in the landscape. They do not blend themselves into the earth but stand separate and unconnected, exerting their own presence. As time passes, I know that this concrete and steel world will expand, and like the plastic bags, will encroach upon the land, its people and their culture. The plastic bags have thankfully been banned from the city, since Zhongdian was renamed Shangri-la, and the land and city is far cleaner now than just a few years ago. The attention on this area by both Chinese and foreign organizations has brought many positive changes that will help pre-serve the vast natural areas that are so unique to China. But, modernity is still approaching with certain inevitability, pushing traditional life back into the past and pulling people away from the earth. Big changes are coming to this small place. I won-der, if I walk up that same mountain in ten years, whether or not incense will still burn there and prayer flags will still manage to fly high above the modern city.

朝聖者

這裡有許多寧靜而簡樸的時光

2000年10月，中旬。我坐在厚實的羊毛毯上烤火。坐在我右邊的老人探身去取一只小小的、被燻黑的茶壺，茶葉在水中上下翻滾，他把茶壺朝燃燒的煤炭堆裡推去。當他的身子向前傾斜時，我看到火焰在他平靜的眼睛裡起舞。左邊的老婦人低聲誦經，佈滿皺紋的粗大手指緩慢而不停地撥弄著木佛珠。隨著起伏的誦經韻律，木珠緩緩轉動，一顆、二顆、三顆……深入體驗某個地方與走馬看花的旅遊大相逕庭。每個地方都有自己獨特的生活節奏，想要瞭解一個地方，必須深入其中，加快或放慢自己的腳步，使自己和這個地方步調一致。城市緊張的生活節奏充斥在空氣中，迫使人們加快腳步。有時，似乎緊張得連呼吸的時間都沒有。

2000. October. Zhongdian. I sit on thick wool carpet and warm my hands over a fire. The old man sitting to my right reaches for the small, blackened pot in which tealeaves are simmering in water and pushes it further into the burning coals. As he leans forward, flames dance in the calm of his eyes. From my left comes the sound of an old woman's soft chanting. Thick, wrinkled fingers slowly make their way over round, wooden beads. The voice rises and falls, the beads turn. One... two...three...To experience a place is something quite different from seeing or touring it. Every place has its own unique pulse and to come into contact with it, one must enter the rhythm of life there, by speeding up or slowing down to synchronize oneself to that place. Cities exist on a staccato pace that seems to fill the air and pushes people to quicken their step. Sometimes, it is as if there is hardly time to breathe.

中甸　藏族之家

小中甸

　　但是在中甸，生活是從容不迫的，這裡有許多寧靜而簡樸的時光，它們似乎使時間緩慢流逝。當我在中甸的時候，我幾乎不會考慮現在是什麼時代，在這裡，100年前可能和現在差不多。時光流逝的意義似乎不大，有時，過去和現在好像重疊在一起。獨處時，這種感覺會特別強烈，我彷彿能夠深切地感受並理解這個地方。當四周都很寧靜時，我依稀能聽到這片土地正對我傾訴著什麼秘密。香格里拉就是這樣一個地方。

In Zhongdian, the pace is unhurried and there are many quiet, simple moments that seem to slow time. There are moments there when I can hardly think of what year it is, for it seems that I could exist within any moment from the past one hundred years. The passing of time seems to have less significance and sometimes a current minute feels as if it is overlapped and filled with remnants of the minutes of the past. In the quiet, those moments are most perceptible and I can really feel the place and understand something of it. In the silence, sometimes, I can hear a place speaking to me. Shangri-la is one of those places.

離開德欽飛來寺的朝聖者

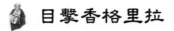

目擊香格里拉

　　2001年3月。一個滿面笑容的人衝我喊道:「歡迎來香格里拉。」他的手裡拿著《消失的地平線》,興奮地指著書的封面說道:「在這裡,你會發現詹姆斯‧希爾頓在他的書裡所描繪的世外桃源。」他帶我離開車站,經過告誡旅遊者要注意小偷的警示牌,來到街道上。剛粉刷過的粉紅色建築前,工人們正仔細地用石頭鋪設一條新的人行道。我不記得詹姆斯‧希爾頓的書裡有沒有粉紅色的百貨商店和城市街道。風吹起的塵土在空中飛舞,一群藏族女人用籃子背著石頭走過,她們用藍色的頭巾遮擋風沙。街對面,一個深膚色的藏族男子背靠著房屋,他的眼睛從牛仔帽下好奇地打量著我。我感覺到空氣中的寒意,以及這個地方的寒冷氣息。

中甸男人

中旬　男孩

2001. March. A smiling man greets me and exclaims, "Welcome to Shangri-la." In his hand he carries the book Lost Horizon. He excitedly points to the cover and says, "Here you will find the paradise that James Hilton described in his book." He turns and leads me out of the bus station past signs posted warning visitors to protect their belongings against potential thieves, and onto the street where workers are carefully setting stones for a new sidewalk in front of freshly painted pink buildings. I don't recall anything about pink department stores, or even city streets in the book. Wind blows dust up in swirls as a group of Tibetan women walk by carrying baskets of stone, their faces shielded from the wind by blue scarves. Across the street, a dark Tibetan man stands against a building, his eyes peering out from under his cowboy hat. I feel a chill in the air and emanating from this place.

小中甸　兄妹

名字，事物與意義

　　漢人為孩子取名字時，名字中包含著他們對孩子的期望。今天，中國在重塑自己，而香格里拉就是中國的新生兒之一。舊中國正退出舞臺，通過一番艱難的修整，新的中國正在廢墟之上建立起來。這是一個強大、光輝的新中國，越來越接近於西方。透過英國作者的筆，「香格里拉」被介紹到中國。中國想要說明的是，西方人觀念中的世外桃源，就是在政治和經濟上與西方往來越來越密切的中國。香格里拉是新中國的一部分，這個名字裡負載著中國的希望和夢想。

　　When Chinese name their children, they give names containing the hopes they hold for the children. Today, China is reinventing itself, and Shangri-la is one of China's newly born. The old is being pushed out, ploughed under, and on top of the rubble, the new China is being built. It is strong, gleaming, and looking more and more like the West. Shangri-la was introduced to China through the writing of an Englishman. How appropriate that China now lays claim to a western mind's paradise just as China looks to build greater political and economic relations with the West. Shangri-la is part of China's rebirth and represents many of the hopes and dreams that this name signifies.

佛教徒對名字卻有不同的看法。對於他們，名字只是一個概念或生命的符號，本身並沒有什麼意義，而且很容易給予和變化，但要改變一個人或一個地方就困難多了。在美國，Kim Roseberry就代表我，而在中國，我卻變成了梅昱熒。我有兩個完全不同且沒有關聯的名字，但卻都是指同一個人。中甸和香格里拉也是意思和含義完全不同的兩個名字，卻也是指向相同的地方。名字只是一個人、一個地方或一個事物的外在符號，並不代表事物的本質。名字是一個語言工具，和時鐘的滴答聲一樣空洞。在這名字之後的東西更重要。在對某個事物或某個人做出判斷時，名字絕對不能當作最重要的標準。

Buddhists take a very different stance on names. For them, a name is merely a representation of a concept or being. A name itself holds nothing and is easy to give and change. To change a person or place is far more difficult. In America, I am known as Kim Roseberry. In China, my name is Mei Yuying. I hold two different, unrelated names, yet I am the same person. Zhongdian and Shangri-la are two names with distinct meanings and implications, yet the place is one. A name is merely something laid on top of a person, place or thing, but contains absolutely no substance of what it is identifying. It is merely a tool of language and is as empty as the tick of a clock. What stands behind the name is of far more importance. A name cannot be held as the most important or significant thing when judging something or someone.

瑪尼堆上的經文

但現在，「香格里拉」這個名字的內涵已經被固定了，這個標題具有人間
天堂的含義。對每個人來說，天堂的意義不盡相同。那是一個一切都盡善盡美
的地方，沒有爭鬥，生活的艱辛消失在祝福和祈禱中。大家的腦海中也許都存
在著某種天堂的觀念。有夢想很正常，但也有少數夢想者，他們認為如果找對
了地方，夢想一定存在於現實世界裡。他們相信人間有天堂，所以他們走遍世
界各個角落去尋找青春之泉、天國和伊甸園。有人相信可以建立一個政治和社
會制度完美的公社——烏托邦。這些勇敢的嘗試最終都失敗了。現在中國也正試
圖在香格里拉創造新的人間天堂，但這卻是一個幾乎不可能完成的任務。當我
走在這個新命名的人間天堂的街道上時，我發現腦海裡和現實中的香格里拉在
激烈衝撞著。

太子廟　擺放油燈的老人，彷彿正在細心地擺放他的信仰

But now, Shangri-la has been located and named, and with the title comes the notion of an earthly paradise. For each person, paradise is something different; it is a place where all things are perfect, where struggle does not exist, where the hardship of life disappears into bliss. Somewhere in the back of everyone's mind there exists some notion of paradise. It is a dream common to man, and there have been those exceptional dreamers who believed that the dream could be found in the real world if one just looked in the right places. They believed in paradise on earth, and so they travelled to the corners of the world searching for the Fountain of Youth, Zion, and Eden. Some believed that they could create Utopia by establishing communities based on a vision of political and social perfection. They were all brave endeavours that ended in failure. China is now attempting to create the newest paradise in Shangri-la and putting itself up to a nearly impossible task. As I stepped out onto the street of the newly named paradise, I found the images of Shangri-la that I had in my head crashing mightily with the reality of what I saw.

山谷中的房屋

將一個地方命名為香格里拉，實際上是剝奪人們的夢想。香格里拉是想像中的天堂，每個人對天堂的觀念不同。天堂是最美好的理想和幻想，如果用香格里拉命名一個地方，那麼天堂就成為一個具體的有形物。將夢想強迫變成現實，等於是毀了這個夢想。人們花費畢生的精力去尋找他們自己的天堂，而當他們來到香格里拉時，就是終結了找尋的過程。不需要再找了，理想和幻想都結束了。神話變成現實。現實無法與夢想相比，我們頭腦中的夢想也不復存在，已經碎了。相信生活可以更自由、更美麗、更平和、更超凡脫俗，是人的一種需要。我們在頭腦中創造的神話和夢想，成為我們逃避現實的避風港。香格里拉，多少年來一直是這樣的一個神話，但是現在卻成為現實；神話消失了，按照自己的觀念來定義香格里拉的那種自由永遠消失了。

中甸　牧人

To name a place Shangri-la is to take away people's dreams. Shangri-la is supposedly paradise, but every person's idea of paradise is different. Para- dise is of dreams and fantasy and by naming and giving a place to that paradise is to de- fine it in concrete terms. To force that dream into reality is to destroy it. People spend their lives searching for their own piece of paradise, and so, to visit Shangri- la is to end that search. There is no need to go on looking and the dream and fantasy are ended. The myth is brought into existence. Most likely, the reality will not live up to the dream, but the dream can no longer exist, and can no longer be visited in our own minds; it is shattered. There is a human need to believe in the possibility of a life that is more fluid, more beautiful, more peaceful, and more transcendent. Myths and the dream worlds we create in our minds offer an escape from reality. Shangri-la, for many years has been such a myth, but now it has been given the reality; the myth can no longer be brought back, and the freedom to define one's own version of Shangri-la is lost.

晨霧中的松贊林寺

來了一隊旅遊者

2001年3月，香格里拉。清晨，我搭乘3路公車去松贊林寺。嘰嘰嘎嘎的車上擠滿人，有繫著藍色圍裙、戴著裝飾著粉紅毛紗和閃光花環的帽子的藏族女人，男人則穿著黑色的藏袍。許多人手上拿著佛珠。下車後，我爬了很多級臺階到主神殿。殿堂裡面，披著栗色袈裟的年長僧人在朗誦經文，不時地敲鼓。我坐在殿堂的邊緣觀察並聆聽他們平靜而有韻律的誦經聲。空氣中透著莊嚴神聖，我謹慎得不敢發出一絲聲響。突然，左邊傳來手提喇叭的聲音，跟著來了一隊遊客。導遊小姐帶領大家進入大廳，隨意指著牆上栩栩如生的宗教繪圖講解著，遊客像是一群鴨子不停地拍照。寧靜被打破，也無法聽到僧侶的誦經。在那一刻，我很同情這些僧人，他們竟然變成吸引旅遊者的物件。

2001. March. Shangri-la. It is early morning and I take the No. 3 bus to the Songzanlin Temple. The rattling bus is crowded with local Tibetan women wearing blue aprons and hats wrapped by pink yarn and glittery garland and men wearing dark-coloured chubas. Many people hold prayer beads in their hands. The bus lets us off and I make my way up the many steps to the main temple. Inside, senior monks wrapped in maroon robes are chanting scriptures and occasionally strike an upright drum. I sit on the edge of the room, watching and listening to the rhythm of their voices in the calmness. Sacredness permeates the air and I am careful not to make a sound. Suddenly, from the left comes the blast of a bullhorn as a tour guide ushers in her followers. She directs them about the hall, pointing out the freshly painted deities on the walls, and as she speaks, the tourists follow her like ducks, snapping pictures as they go. The serenity of the previous moment is lost and the monks' prayers can no longer be heard. I feel for the monks who, in that moment, are reduced to a tourist draw.

中旬　松贊林寺　祈禱

他們必須生活在旅遊者的夢想裡

命名香格里拉也爲本地人帶來很大的壓力。現在
他們必須生活在旅遊者的夢想裡。他們不能按照
過去的方式生活，而要依照外來人的想法生活。
找尋夢中樂園的人蜂擁而至，當地人必須試著滿
足旅人的需求。他們開始生活在一種虛構之中，
就像在舞臺上表演的演員，不再爲自己活著，而
是爲觀衆存在。甚至就連最純粹、最神聖的人和
場所也成爲這樣的演員和舞臺。

The name Shangri-la puts extreme pressure on its own people. Now, the local people must attempt to live up to the dreams of the visitors. They cannot go on living their lives as before, but must now consider and mould their lives to the ideals that out-siders carry in their minds. The crowds roll in anxiously searching for a dreamland and the locals must try and offer it to them. The local people begin to live in fiction, per-forming as actors on a stage, living no longer for themselves, but for their audience and even the purest, most sacred of people and places are made to perform.

在聚會上

　　2002年。新年之夜。中甸。吃喝停了下來，唱歌開始了。有兩個人信口唱起了流行歌曲，大家愉快地鼓掌。然後，一個高大的藏族男子站起來。他的皮膚因日曬而呈棕褐色，與眼睛的白色部分形成鮮明的對比。當第一聲響聲在他胸中醞釀，再從他的口中逸出時，所有人都把目光對準了他，大家震撼了。時間彷彿停滯下來。他的眼睛緊閉，好像在思考詞句，而歌聲則像是從我們目光無法抵達的遙遠地方傳過來似的。歌聲如洪水般淹沒我的全身，我不禁開始顫抖。他的聲音純粹得像清冷的水，同時又凝聚著幾個世紀以來的西藏戰士的力量，刺透了寂靜。歌聲逐漸消失，一種似可觸摸的靜默重新注滿整個房間。他彎腰坐下，吱吱作響的椅子打破平靜。他舉手指著我，要我唱。但他唱得太好，我不敢接著唱。不唱就必須喝酒。我起身將一杯白酒一飲而盡，酒杯輕輕地放在桌上，然後坐下。

2002. New Years Eve. Zhongdian. The eating has stopped and the singing has begun. A couple of people stand and deliver their own renditions of popular songs, which are followed by cheerful clapping. Then, a tall Tibetan man stands up. His skin is tanned a leathery brown from the sun and the whites of his eyes stand out in sharp contrast. As the first sound rises from his chest and escapes from between his lips, everybody's eyes turn to him, transfixed. Time stops. His eyes are closed and it is as if he is drawing words and sound from some faraway place we cannot see. Shivers flow through me as his voice rings through the silence with purity like that of glacial water and strength of centuries of Tibetan fighters. The sound fades and then a tangible silence flows back in to fill the room. The man bends at the waist and sits, the creak of the chair shattering the moment. His hand raises and points to me. I stand, empty a glass of baijiu down my throat, place the glass on the table with a soft clink and sit down.

中甸　男人和女人

稍後，西方的音樂撞擊著耳朵，那種振動穿透身體。我站在閃爍的燈光下翩翩起舞。黑色藏族人的面孔包圍著我。我突然想起朋友曾經對我說過，幾年前這裡有過謀殺的事情。兩個人為了搶佔長有蘑菇的土地而發生爭鬥，後來其中一個死了。我扭動、旋轉、轉身。幾個長髮的男子手裡握著棕色瓶子盛裝的百威啤酒。許多人看著我，試圖模仿我跳舞的樣子。他們旋轉時，腰間的長刀在燈光下發亮。等到他們的臉轉過來時，我看到了某種茫然。

Later that night, Western music pounds in my ears and vibrates through my body. I stand in the flashing lights and begin to dance. Dark Tibetan faces surround me. I think of what my friend has just told me of the murder that occurred a few years ago. Two men had a dispute over mushroom territory and one ended up dead. I move, I spin, I turn. Some of the longhaired men clasp brown bottles of Budweiser beer in their hands. Many people watch me, and try to imitate my movements. As they spin, light glances off the hilt of the long knives held at their backs. As their faces come around, I see looks of uncertainty.

中甸　燈光下的藏族婦女

藏族漢子

藏族是一個自豪的民族，他們一代又一代地在世界上最艱難的環境中生存，所以其生命力具有一種罕見的力量。歷史上，藏族出過一些最勇敢的戰士和最可怕的強盜。在藏族男子唱歌的晚上，我意識到了這種力量。有時，在我旅行時，人們會展示出自身的特質，這種特質是如此特別以致於我迷失其中而不能自拔。2002年元旦的晚上，就是這樣的時刻。藏族人不會為了這一天而特別慶賀，但那個唱歌的男子卻完全控制在場所有人。他的嗓音裡迴盪著一種無庸置疑的真實和信心，完全征服了我。但在其後的晚上，我卻看到一些完全不同的事情。在跳迪斯可時，我發現一些藏族人嘗試將他們過去的歷史和外來的事物融合在一起，他們做得十分笨拙。當他們喝著洋酒並努力跟上音樂的節奏時，他們從祖先身上繼承的精神已然殞落。我看到一種力量的失去，但它在那天晚上一開始還是真實地存在著。

中甸　牲畜交易市場
藏族男人騎在賽馬上

Tibetans are a proud people, and carry within their beings a rare strength that is drawn from generations of living in one of the world's harshest environments. They have been some of the history's bravest fighters and most fear- some bandits. As the Tibetan man sang that night, I witnessed that strength . Occasionally, in my travels, there are times when people exhibit something so extraordinary that I am lost in the moment and have difficulty gathering myself after it has passed. New Year's Eve that year was one of those times. Tibetans do not typically celebrate the day, and yet, this man took complete control of the evening and the people in front of him. His voice rang with unchallengeable truth and confidence, and left me with nothing with which to answer. Though, later that evening, I witnessed something quite different. In the disco, watching some Tibetan men trying to reconcile their historic past with the oncoming foreign present was to see them stumble. As they drank foreign alcohol and tried to move themselves to foreign rhythms, they were letting go of some of the spirit that has carried the previous generations, and through that compromise, I saw a loss of the strength that had rung so true earlier that evening.

曾是天生的舞蹈家

　　2003年9月。居加村。我們受到載歌載舞的年輕男女歡迎，他們穿著華麗藏服，唱著「歡迎！歡迎！」，舉著鑲嵌著銀絲的木酒杯向我們敬酒，然後獻給我們哈達。一條陡峭的小路通向村莊，籃球場邊擺著為我們準備的桌子和椅子，一場精心準備的表演將展開。村子專門為我們舉辦的這個儀式讓我感到不安。一隊男子走上前，踏腳轉身，開始唱聖歌。接著，婦女向前，轉圈，長長的袖子舞成優美的弧線。

居加村　盛裝的年輕人　一場精心準備的表演

　　2003. September. Jujia Village. We are welcomed by dancing young men and women dressed in flashy Tibetan costumes singing "Welcome! Welcome!" We are offered baijiu served in wooden cups lined in silver and our shoulders are adorned with katas. We are led down a steep path to the village below where a table and chairs have been set up for us on the edge of the basketball court where a performance has been prepared. I am a little embarrassed at the lengths the village has gone to for our group. A line of men come forward, stomping and turning, their voices joined in chant. The women advance, spinning, their long sleeves arching in graceful circles.

來自居加村的女孩，以盛在飾有銀邊的木杯中的白酒歡迎我們

最初，我有點沮喪，因爲這些舞蹈像是只爲了遊客而表演的。但我環顧四周，發現所有的村民都在這裡，老人們微笑地坐在球場邊的土埂上。我聽見村裡的年長者說，村民爲了這一天工作了四年。有幾十年沒有人跳這種舞，幾乎失傳了。現在要發展觀光，地方官員要求復興傳統舞蹈，叫那些還記得傳統舞步的老人教年輕人。當老人們坐在土埂上時，他們驕傲地看著辛苦的果實。也許他們想起了自己年輕時的意氣風發，當時他們身體強壯柔軟，是天生的舞蹈家。

居加村　看年輕人跳舞的老人

At first, I feel a little dismayed that this dance was like a performance for tourists, but then I look around. The entire village is here, and the old people sit on the bank above the court smiling broadly. I learn from one of the village leaders that the people of Jujia have been practicing this presentation for four years. The dance steps have not been performed for decades and are nearly lost. With the prospect of tourism building, the area officials decided to promote the resurrection of the dance tradition and called upon the old people who still remembered the traditional dances to teach the younger people. As the elders sit up on that bank, they are proudly seeing the fruit of their efforts and perhaps remembering their younger years when their bodies were limber and they were the dancers.

中甸　藏族新娘和她的女儐相

人們為什麼要來香格里拉

　　2003年9月，中旬。通往松贊林寺的公路旁有一個休息處。一扇小門和標誌牌吸引遊客來到舞臺佈景的場所。在這裡可以和穿著鮮豔藏族傳統服裝、抱著雪白可愛羊羔的女孩合影，背景是有名的寺廟。只要「唭嚓」一聲按下快門，就可以捕捉到最典型的「香格里拉」——具異國情調、穿著美麗服裝的女人，存在於神秘土地上的藏傳佛教，以及人類與自然的完美和諧。遊客也可以自己穿上藏服，抱著羊羔站在佈景前拍照，然後向親友炫耀自己是如何與神秘的香格里拉融合在一起的。或者，他們也可以拍攝站在一旁的滿臉鬍鬚的高大男子，和他那頭仔細梳理過的犛牛。這個男人和他的犛牛出現在若干有關香格里拉的書籍和畫冊裡。拍攝和捕捉這片遙遠大地野性精神的照片只需要5元。花點小錢，你就可以擁有香格里拉，拿回家放在相簿裡。我沒有在這個抱著羔羊的女人前停步，而是將鏡頭對準山下一個趕著犛牛耕地的男人。

在居加村

在白水台
鏡頭和這片土地上的人們
李玉祥／攝

　　2003. September. Zhongdian. On the way to the Songzanlin Monastery is a stop along theroad. A small gate and sign lure tourists to a scenic spot where they can take photos of girls wearing flashy Tibetan costumes holding perfectly white fluffy lambs against the backdrop of the famous temple. In one click of the shutter, one can capture a popular version of Shangrila - exotic, beautifully dressed women, living in the mysterious land of Tibetan Buddhism, and existing in harmony with nature. Tourists can also put on the costume, hold the innocent little lamb and insert themselves into this scene and produce a photograph that they can show all their friends that exhibits how they truly integrated themselves with the mysterious Shangri-la. Or, they can photograph the tall, bearded man standing nearby with his carefully combed woolly yak. It is the same man and yak featured in several books on Shangri-la. Take their photo and capture the wild spirit of this faraway land. All this for about five yuan. Spend five yuan and you can possess Shangri-la, take it home with you and put it in a photo album. I make my way past the women with the fluffy lambs and focus my camera on a man and his yaks ploughing the field below.

看著這一切，我不禁自問：人們爲什麼要來香格里拉？好像它是一個刻意的安排，一個許多人尋找的一種確實可見的形象，而不是一種經歷。所謂經歷，就是需要透過努力才能到達的地方，而且還要眞正進去！眞正進入需要付出努力，要把自己的心房向當地的人民、風光和文化完全敞開，並理解他們。但是，只索取而不給予，無法眞正進入嚮往的任何地方。雖然給予很困難，但這是與人或地方進行交流的必要條件，這需要時間、努力和溝通。唯有透過交流，才算眞正體驗一個地方，也才能眞正融入那個地方。

小活佛贈送哈達

Seeing such a place, I ask, for what reason do people come to Shangri-la? It seems that it is a setting, and an image that many are seeking, not an experience. It takes effort to go to a place and really enter it. To enter a place is to open oneself to the people, landscape, and culture and then to absorb some of it. But, in order to receive, one must also be willing to give and this is what prevents so many from ever entering any of the places they go. Giving is difficult but necessary in any exchange with a person or place, and it requires time, effort, and a willingness to communicate. Only through communication does one really experience a place, and only when communication is achieved can one learn something about that place and truly experience it.

中甸　在公路邊遇到了一位藏族婦女。李玉祥／攝

　　但是對許多人來說，他們只需要有一個來到某地的證明，理解是次要的。因此，正如其他所有的旅遊景點一樣，香格里拉提供的僅是這樣一種需求：只要給錢，馬上就可以獲得來到這個遙遠地方所希望得到的神秘和冒險。只要付一點錢，就可以和一位懷抱羔羊、穿著漂亮服裝、具異國情調的女孩合影，以此作為香格里拉之旅的證明。每一件事都如此簡單，不需和女孩交談，也不需要理解她，更不需敞開自己。只要女孩微笑，遊客微笑，然後共同拍攝一張美麗而空洞的照片。

But, for many, it is enough to merely hold evidence that one wasin such a place; understanding is secondary. And, so, as all touristspots do, Shangri-la offers something that only requires giving the thing that is easiest to give - money - but captures all the mystery and adventure one would hope for in travelling to such a faraway place. For a little money, one can take a picture with an exotic girl with her lambs, in a beautiful setting that will represent the entire journey through the land. Everything is made so easy. There is no need to talk to her, to understand her, or to give anything of one's self. The girl smiles, the tourist smiles and together they make a beautiful, empty picture.

中甸村莊

俯視虎跳峽。　李玉祥／攝

視覺上的有限尺度

　　2003年9月，中旬。我懷疑旅伴們是不是被相機蒙蔽了。我們站在路邊，目光掠過腳下峽谷，看到遠方壯麗巍峨的雪山。每一個人都拿起相機，焦點放在鏡頭裡，不停地按動腳架上的相機，然後很快收工汽車。我沒有跟隨他們，而是靠著冰冷的岩石坐下來，在清爽的微風和清新的空氣中凝視著眼前遼闊的群山，感覺自己非常渺小但又異常清醒。車門關上，我聽不到裡面的交談。除了風聲，一片寂靜。背對著車子，有那麼一剎那，我感覺我是獨自一人，但非常平靜。

　　我們繼續旅程，繼續搜索覆蓋深秋火紅的低矮灌木的曠野。眼前是巨大通紅的碎片。我來到原野，大步快走。紅是血、火和愛的顏色。我企望投入它的懷抱，吸收它的活力。我真希望躺臥在火一般燃燒的大地上，注視著澄藍的天空—這是血管、流水和寧靜的顏色。然而，身邊的相機提醒我還有工作，時間是有限的。

中旬

2003. September. Zhongdian. I wonder if my companions have been blinded by their cameras. We stand on the side of the road, high above a valley, looking across at magnificent and massive snow-covered mountains. Each person sets up their camera, looks through the frame and takes several photos. Finished, the others quickly climb into the van. I do not follow them, but sit outside on a cold rock feeling the brisk wind against my face and breathing the fresh air. I stare at the vast mountains before me, feeling small and feeling awake. The van door is closed and I cannot hear the conversation inside. It is silent except for the sound of the wind. My back is turned to the van, and, for a moment, I am alone in that place. I am at peace. On we travel, searching for fields aglow with the autumnal red of the low bushes. With my eyes upon the largest, reddest patch, I set out into the field, walking as fast as my legs can carry me. Red, the colour of blood, fire, and love. I want to be swallowed by it, to absorb some of its energy. I want to lie in that field of fire and stare up at the blue, blue sky, the colour of veins, water, and tranquillity. But, then I remember the camera at my side and my assignment. Time is limited.

德欽　藏式建築

對我來說，拍攝一張照片絕不能說就捕獲了這個地方。每個地方都在不停地運動、變化著，具有鮮活的生命。每當我進入一片動人的風景時，我就會和它有一種互動關係。我站著和它交流，被它所環繞。對我來說，體驗一個地方不只是到實地去看，還要感受吹在臉上的風，聆聽湍急的流水，呼吸清新的空氣。一張照片只捕獲這種經驗某一個方面的有限視野。即使是相同的地方，不同的人也會有不同的經驗和感受。每個人對問題的判斷和理解是不一樣的。

承恩寺　小活佛和年長的朋友

　　For me, a photo can never truly capture a place. A place is in motion, constantly changing, and alive. When I step into a landscape, I am interacting with it. I stand in relation to it, and am surrounded by it. For me to experience a landscape is not only to see the actual place, but also to feel the wind on my face, to hear rushing water, to smell the clarity of the air. A photo can only capture a limited view of one dimension of this experience. Two people in the same place will have to separate experiences for what their senses pick up will be different.

虎跳峽　瀑布

身旁的人也許注意到圍繞著山頂的雲像是一張毯子，但我注意到的卻是從雪山山頂奔流到綠色峽谷的小河。也許我們拍攝的是幾乎一模一樣的照片，但我們看待這個地方的方式卻完全不同。沒有人能瞥一眼就完全把握住此地的一切，而必須到處遊覽，注意每個細節。每個人觀察的角度都是獨特的，都帶著自己的背景和經驗去理解某個地方。過去和現在密不可分，我們過去看待事物的方式，對今天依然有著影響。選擇的角度，應該強調事物的某些部分，無論是忽視或希望獲得的部分，都影響著我們觀察的心態。

The person beside me may notice the way clouds wrap themselves around the peak of a mountain is like a blanket. And maybe I notice the line of a small river running down from the mountain and how it connects the snowy peak to the green valley. Perhaps we would take nearly identical pictures, but the way in which we saw the place was completely different. One does not glimpse a place and take it all in at once, but instead, moves through it, noticing one part and then another. Each person's procession is unique, for each of us brings our own background and experience to that place. The current moment is never separate from the previous, and our past affects the way in which we see today. The angle we take, the things we choose to focus upon, the things we ignore and what we hope to gain all influence the way we see.

香格里拉是中國最有視覺衝擊力的地方之一。秋天，原野呈現壯闊的紅色，當太陽接近地平線時，陽光投射在大地上，矮灌木看起來似乎在燃燒。太陽移動時，雄偉的山脈會變爲深紫色。藍色的水反映微光，變幻出彩虹般的色澤。深藍的天空映襯著栗色和金色的寺廟。閃爍炫目純白光芒的雪山，在落日的餘暉中轉爲柔和的粉紅色。很少能在一個地方看見如此豐富多彩的景象。當地居民的表情也值得玩味，大地的險峻和美麗都反射在每個人臉上，彷彿融化在他們生活之中。當我來到這裡時，我的眼睛搜索著每個地方，拿出相機時激動不已。有時，相機會佔用我過多的時間，我發現自己甚至忘記應該騰出多一點時間來理解這個地方。我不得不收起相機。有時，我只是拍攝照片，對拍攝什麼沒有感覺，只是用眼睛來感受，而不是用其他的感官來感受。

中甸　納帕海

Shangri-la is one of the most visually stimulating places in China. In the fall, the fields are swaths of bright red, and when the sun lowers in the sky and the light is cast at sharp angles across the land, the short bushes seem to be on fire. As the sun sets, the imposing mountains turn a deep purple and water an iridescent blue. Temples of maroon and gold stand against deep skies of navy and the snow that covers the mountains is of a blindingly pure white that changes to soft pinks at sundown. Rarely does one find a place so full of colour. The people there are equally eyecatching. It seems

that the land, in all of its ruggedness and beauty, is reflected in their faces and they are one with the place they live. When I enter such a place, my eye is sent everywhere, and excitement fills me as I take out my camera. Sometimes, though, the camera has a way of overtaking my time in a place and I find myself forgetting to take a few moments to really take in the place and I have to put the camera down. Otherwise, I will only have photographs, but no impression in my mind and will have only experienced the place with my eyes and not the rest of my senses.

Kim Roseberry的父親

土地上的卑微居民

　　2003年9月，中旬。我注視著香格里拉誠實的面容。透過鏡頭，我看到一個女孩拉著兩頭犛牛艱難向前，她的父親在後面，握著在佈滿砂石的土地上耕種著的犁。女人提著籃子，用粗糙的雙手在土地裡尋找土豆。當我走向他們時，他們因為衣服的骯髒感到窘迫，而轉過身背對著我。這就是那些居住在中國官方命名為「香格里拉」的土地上的卑微的居民。這裡既沒有清澈透亮的水晶石，也沒有閃爍的黃銅，只有泥土和石頭。我看不到奢華，只看到辛苦的勞動。剎時，我想到在自己的農場拼命做事的父親。我按下快門，然後上車。

2003. September. Zhongdian. I am standing in Shangri-la looking at its honest face. Through my camera lens I am framing a young girl leading two yaks through a rough field. Her father walks behind, guiding the plough through the rocky soil. Women with baskets dig through the soil, pulling potatoes from the earth with their thick fingers. As I turn to them, they turn their backs in embarrassment at their dirty clothes. These are the humble residents of China's officially named Shangri-la. There is neither crystal nor shining brass, only earth and stone. I see no luxury here; I see toil. For a second, I think of my father back home, working his farm. My shutter clicks and I step into the van.

牽犛牛的女孩

車子發動時，我思考著承受香格里拉盛名壓力的這塊土地，我思考著車上的其他人，也思考著生活在這塊土地上的人。這樣一個地方，我們有著不同的看法。我的夥伴們大部分都來自擁擠、現代的城市街道。他們來自由混凝土和鋼筋把他們和土地及大自然分割開來的那個地方，來自非常昂貴的空間。而這裡廣闊的原野上只點綴零星的房屋，背靠冰雪覆蓋的群山。相對於車上的同伴，這裡是令人欣喜的地方。但是對於田地上的人來說，卻只有艱苦耕作的土地。他們在這片大地工作，食物來自這片大地，連房屋的材料都來自這片大地。另外，這塊土地也將他們束縛在貧窮之中，遠離現代世界。不過，我想：每件事物的樣貌端視觀察的角度而定。

居加村　老人

As the van moves on I think of this land that bears the name of Shangri-la. I think of the other people in the vehicle and then of the people who live on this land. It is one place, but we all see it differently. My companions largely come from the crowded, modern city streets. They live in a place of concrete and steel that separates them from the earth and nature, a place where space is an expensive commodity. For them, this wide-open land dotted with occasional houses and back dropped by snow-covered mountains is refreshing. The people in the fields have known nothing but the earth. They work it, their food comes from it, and their homes are built of it. In some ways, this land is a fetter that keeps them in poverty and out of the modern world. Everything is a matter of perspective.

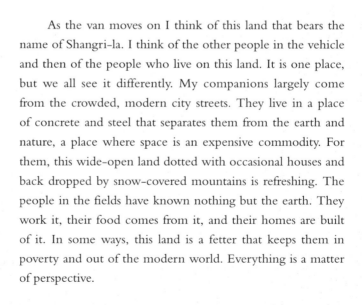

中甸　原野上的村莊

耕作歸來

我懷疑，生活在香格里拉的人是否認為自己生活在人間天堂。遊客把這裡描繪得如天堂般和諧。對於外來者而言，在土地上耕作的人成為風景的一部分，就像一座山或一條河。距離使我們對這裡產生奢侈的美感。我們到這裡來只觀看一種外在的美。大部分的人都不在乎隱藏在這美麗面孔之後的種種細節。當我告訴人們我在一個廣闊土地的農場長大時，他們會說：「我要是能生活在那裡該有多幸福啊！」但是我的成長根本不是那麼一回事。在我離開農場後，我才能欣賞它。只有從外面看時，香格里拉才是天堂，和我的農場一樣。從內部看，就完全不同了。這裡的居民生活在一種人與自然親密的關係之中。他們的生活是現實的，不是浪漫化。身為過客，我們不需要為了生存而每天和大自然搏鬥，所以我們可以看到它最迷人的一面。

中甸　藏族女孩

I highly doubt that people who live in Shangri-la would call it paradise, but, for the tourists passing through, the people represent a paradisiacal harmony between man and earth. To the outsider, the people working the fields become part of the scenery, like a mountain or river. That is the luxury that distance gives us. It is that exterior model of beauty that we come to see. Most people do not care to know the details behind the face. When I tell people that I grew up on a farm with expansive land, many people exclaim how happy I must have been there. Growing up, that was hardly the case. Only after I left, was I able to appreciate it. Like my farm, Shangri-la is only heavenly when seen from the outside. Seen from the inside, it is something quite different. The residents live within a true and intimate relationship between man and nature; they live the reality, not the romanticized version. As visitors, we are not battling the natural world everyday to make a living, and so we have the freedom to see only its most attractive aspects.

中甸

現代世界成功地把我們和土地分開。人們不是透過橡膠鞋底和混凝土樓層，而是透過自己的雙腳來感受大地的存在。大部分的人也許根本不記得最後一次這麼做是什麼時候的事了。有多少人知道誰生產我們吃的食物？或者這些食物是從什麼地方來的？當我們興高采烈地吃著東西時，我們從來不會費心去想餐桌上食物的種種。霓虹燈將黑暗從城市中驅逐出去。有多少人看過滿天的星星？污濁的空氣和城市的燈光遮蔽了我們的視線。有多少人知道躺臥在原野上睡覺是何種滋味？我們總是希望減輕衝擊來保護柔軟的身體。坐在絕對寂靜的空間聆聽自然夜晚的聲音是什麼滋味？人們甚至不知道如何沉默。對於某些人來說，如果沒有被聲音包圍、沒有朋友陪伴、沒有片刻的娛樂，都是不舒服的。

The modern world does a good job at separating us from the earth. How long has it been since the average person has felt the earth under their feet, not through layers of rubber and concrete? Most people probably could not remember the last time. How many of us produce the actual food we eat, or even know where it comes from? We eat gaily with never a thought for the people who produce the food for our table. Neon lights banish the darkness from cities. How many of us can see the millions of stars in the night sky? Pollution and city lights cloud our view. How many of us know what it feels like to sleep on the ground? We demand cushioning to protect our soft bodies. What is it like to sit in complete silence and listen to nature's night sounds? People hardly know how to be silent. For some, it is an uneasy feeling to not be surrounded by the sound and presence of humankind, without every moment filled with some distraction.

我思考自己和大地的關係，思考雙方如何被分離。孩提時代，我光腳在牲口棚和原野上奔跑，在草地上追逐蛇，用手抓青蛙，而且經常和母親外出撿漿果和野蘑菇。多少個夜晚，在漫天繁星下露營。現在，我的腳掌已經變得柔軟，我也忘記上次漿果染紅雙手是什麼時候的事了。

　　I think about my own relationship to the earth and how separated I have become. As a child, I ran barefoot through the barns and fields, chased snakes through the grass and caught frogs with my bare hands. I used to go out and pick berries and wild mushrooms with my mother to eat with dinner, and spent many nights camping out under the stars. Now, the soles of my feet have grown soft, and I can't remember the last time my hands were stained red from berries.

緬因州　農場

　　儘管我們在現代樓層裡舒適地生活，但是現代生活卻包圍我們，迫使我們和大自然分開。然而，內心深處渴望和自然世界相連，是人類的本能：聆聽悅耳的激流聲，在山巔眺望遠方，撫摸苔蘚，呼吸清新的空氣和森林深處的氣息。這些與大自然相連的時刻，讓人愉悅。當我還是個孩子時，我是大自然的一部分，這種認知存在於我的心底。但我發現，當人們年歲漸長，許多人，包括我自己，試圖並努力要在成人世界掙得一席之地時，這種認知就被壓抑而遺忘了。不過，希望和大自然在一起的野性，仍然存在我的心中，因為它吸引我來到像香格里拉這樣的地方。在這裡我可以感受到自己和周圍環境緊密結合，如同孩子在大地上自由自在地奔跑。

Despite the cushioning that our lives have given us, somewhere inside, underneath the layers of modernity is the natural being which longs to be in contact with the natural world. It is the part of the self that feels joy at the sound of rushing water, the sight of massive mountain peaks, the feel of moss, the taste of fresh air and the smell of a deep forest. The joy comes because, at that moment, we are connecting with the natural world. For me, this inside being was very present as a child, but I have discovered that as people grow older, many of us, including myself, push that part of us down and even begin to forget it as we try and make our place in the human world. Yet, that natural being is still alive and draws me to places like Shangrila where I can still find that connection between my inner self and the environment and I can feel that child that used to run so freely.

中甸　藏族女孩

2003年10月，德欽。老婦人孤獨地站著。她穿著紫色藏服，腰間繫手工紡織的條紋圍裙，衣服佈滿灰塵而呈灰色，頭髮長期沒有梳理而蓬亂。她從掛在肩上的包裡拿出三炷香，慢慢走向火堆，小心點燃並插在灰燼上。合掌後退幾步，祈禱並唱聖歌。雙膝跪下，手掌觸地，然後頭觸地。接著，慢慢站起來，再跪下，手、頭觸地，反覆數次。她周圍無數祈禱用的經幡呈縱橫交錯的蛛網狀，交織成一個神聖的空間。祈禱完後，她轉身準備離開。這時右邊出現一個拿相機的男人，他看到老婦人剛才的祈禱。他拉著她，要她再這樣磕頭。老婦人按照要求再次跪在地上。攝影師也跟著跪下，但卻是為了取最佳的拍攝角度。幾個攝影師跟著過來。老婦人結束第二輪祈禱後，轉身準備離開。攝影師們還是不停地要求老她重複同樣的動作，因為他們需要拍攝。老婦人搖搖頭，笑著走了。我在這群攝影師中間，看著她消失在經幡之中。我為自己感到羞愧。

在這條路上死亡是一種榮譽

2003.October. Deqin. An old woman stands alone. She wears a purple Tibetan dress and a woven striped apron. Her clothing is grey from dust, and her hair is wild from weeks of not being combed. From a bag slung around her shoulders, she pulls out three sticks of incense. She slowly walks to the small open fireplace and carefully lights the incense and stands it in the ash. She steps back with her palms held in prayer and begins to chant. She drops to her knees; her palms touch the ground, and then her forehead. She stands up, and drops again, and again. Surrounding her are thousands of prayer flags strung in a criss-cross web that create the walls and roof of this holy space. She finishes her prayers and turns to leave. From the right comes a man who has just witnessed her act of devotion with a camera. He pulls her back and asks her to repeat her knowtows. She does as she is asked and drops to the ground again. The photographer kneels as well, but to catch the right angle through his lens. Another photographer approaches, and another. She has finished her second round of prayers and turns to leave once again. The photographers ask her to repeat it one more time for their cameras. She shakes her head, smiles and walks away. I was one of those photographers, and watching her disappear among the prayer flags. I feel a little ashamed of myself.

梅里雪山　叩拜雪山之神

背誦經文並轉動轉經筒

這年，許多藏人要花幾個星期圍繞著梅里雪山朝聖──稱爲轉山。每走一步，就要磕頭。每一步，頭都須觸地。他們攜帶的東西僅夠路上吃，完全沒有現代生活般舒適。轉山路是一條艱難的旅途，死神等待著因虛弱而倒下的人。對於藏族人而言，在這條路上死亡是一種榮譽。他們已經到過聖地，做好死亡的準備。死亡只爲一個理由──信仰。在展示他們偉大的信仰之後，他們將離開他們現世的生命，他們深信來世會擁有一個更美好的生活。

This is the year when many Tibetans walk for weeks to make a pilgrimage around Meili Snow Mountain. Some kow-tow, touching their head to the ground at each step. They carry everything they need for survival with them, but nothing of the comforts of modern life. The path around the mountain is a difficult one and death lingers, waiting for the weak to fall. For a Tibetan, to die along this path is glorious, for they have come and may die for one reason - belief. They will leave this life at the time they are displaying their greatest faith and will be reborn into a better next life.

藏族村莊　白塔

信仰

　　一個女人在山前躬身祈禱，在山神面前展示自己的信仰、自己的宗教，她所做旅行的重要意義，以此獲得更偉大、更崇高的存在可能性。我們按下快門，希望捕捉信仰。我們知道展示在眼前的一切是非常珍貴的。很少有人可以為信仰獻身，承受苦難，特別是我們一生都無法理解的事物。現代的視角通常只關注眼前，很少注視明天。

梅里雪山前的朝聖者

　　As the woman bows before the mountain, she displays her belief in the god of the mountain, her religion, the importance of the journey that she has made and the possibility of a greater and higher existence. As the shutters click, the attempt is made to capture that belief. We recognize the rare quality of what is displayed before us. Very few of us believe in something enough to deprive ourselves, to put ourselves through physical suffering, especially for something that will not be realized in this lifetime. The modern vision focuses on the present and rarely extends into tomorrow.

中旬 藏族女孩

許多人一生都沒有信仰，因為這是最容易丟失的東西。挫折、不幸、厄運等使我們的信仰逐漸消失。稍不留意，信仰就會悄悄溜走，消失在生活的混亂之中。我們懷抱著信仰來到世上，而孩子是最虔誠的信仰者。首先，任何事情都是可能的，這個世界充滿許多美好的事物等待被發現。然後，我們教育孩子夢想和童話不是真實的，世界不總是一個友好的地方。當我們還是孩子時，總是好奇地尋找著生命中一切美好的東西。等到長大，卻開始看到事物壞的一面，慢慢地，我們最初美好的信仰消失了。如果不夠堅持，信仰很快就會消失，因為幾乎沒有人教授我們如何堅定信仰。

Belief is something many people lack in their lives, for it is one of the easiest thing to lose. Setbacks, adversity, and misfortune all pry at the belief we hold on to. If we are not careful, it can slip away from us and be lost in the tangle that is life. In the beginning, we start with plenty of belief and, therefore, children are the greatest believers. At first, everything is possible and the world is full of good things to be discovered. Then, slowly, we teach children that dreams and fairytales are not true, that this world is not always a friendly place. As children, we are curious, looking for all the good things in life, and then, as we grow older, we start seeing the bad things, and slowly, our belief in good starts to slip away. If we are not careful, our belief is soon lost, for hardly anybody teaches us how to hold on to belief.

德欽　飛來寺　朝聖者與轉經筒

差異

　　2003年10月，德欽。傳說梅里雪山只對虔誠
的人展示其真實面目。我將相機安在三腳架上，
四周擠滿攝影師和遊客。大家仰望雪山等待著，
但是視線被緊鎖山巔的雲霧遮擋了。於是大家開
始議論天氣，說如果雲層移動一點就可以看到山
峰了。慢慢地、慢慢地，高聳的山峰果真顯露出
來。歡呼聲和按下快門的「哧嚓」聲響成一片。
每個人保持彎腰的姿態，透過鏡頭觀察目標，不
停地拍攝、拍攝，底片盒撒滿一地。當最好的拍
攝時刻到來時，我聽到滿足的讚歎聲，但我只拍
攝幾張就停下來來。

　　2003.October. Deqin. It is said that the mountain only reveals itself to good people. I stand with my
camera set on my tripod. To my right, to my left,
behind me and in front of me are photographers and
tourists. We all face Meili Snow Mountain. We are all
waiting. The clouds pass over the peak, blocking the
tip from our view. People around me begin talking to
the sky, asking the clouds to just shift a little so they
can see the peak. Slowly, slowly, the sharp point
emerges. Cheers rise up from the crowd and shutters
click furiously. People are bent in rigid postures peering through lenses shooting, shooting, shooting. Film
boxes and canisters litter the ground around them. I
hear cries of satisfaction as the moment is captured on
film. I take a few photos and then stop.

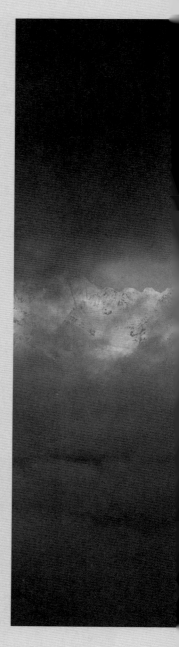

從雲霧之中逐漸浮現的梅里雪山

As I am collapsing my tripod, I see the Tibetan pilgrims below us doing their circumambulations of the white stupas. They appear not to notice the moment that had just brought gleeful cheers. The people above stand anxiously trying to capture the moment, the people below continue to circle and pray, showing no bursts of excitement. Round and round they go, each steadfast step followed by another on a journey of many more steps. We are all in the same place, all searching for something from the mountain, but we are searching for very different things.

在收相機腳架時，我看到山下藏族朝聖者正圍繞著一座白塔朝拜。他們並沒有注意到因為雲層離開雪山而引起的歡呼。上面的人急切地拍攝難得的鏡頭，下面的人則繼續他們的轉山和祈禱，沒有絲毫的激動。他們走了一圈又一圈，在漫長的旅途中，一個堅定的腳步跟著另外一個堅定的腳步。我想，此時此刻所有在場的人，包括轉山的藏民，都站在同樣的地方，都想從山上找到一些東西，但我們找的東西卻不一樣。

梅里雪山　轉山的朝聖者

關係・旅遊者

梅里雪山　卡瓦格博峰

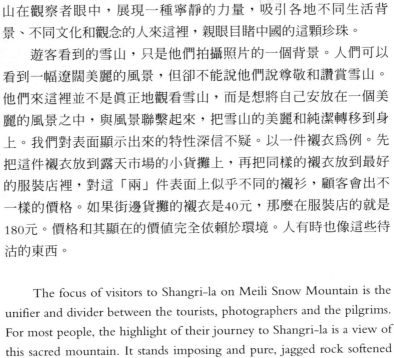

來香格里拉看梅里雪山，使遊客、攝影師和朝聖者之間的看法統一而又分離。對大部分的人來說，來香格里拉旅遊的重點是觀看這座神聖的山峰。皚皚白雪柔和地覆蓋在鋸齒般的岩石山顛上，顯得更加壯麗純潔。雪山在觀察者眼中，展現一種寧靜的力量，吸引各地不同生活背景、不同文化和觀念的人來這裡，親眼目睹中國的這顆珍珠。

遊客看到的雪山，只是他們拍攝照片的一個背景。人們可以看到一幅遼闊美麗的風景，但卻不能說他們說尊敬和讚賞雪山。他們來這裡並不是真正地觀看雪山，而是想將自己安放在一個美麗的風景之中，與風景聯繫起來，把雪山的美麗和純潔轉移到身上。我們對表面顯示出來的特性深信不疑。以一件襯衣為例。先把這件襯衣放到露天市場的小貨攤上，再把同樣的襯衣放到最好的服裝店裡，對這「兩」件表面上似乎不同的襯衫，顧客會出不一樣的價格。如果街邊貨攤的襯衣是40元，那麼在服裝店的就是180元。價格和其顯在的價值完全依賴於環境。人有時也像這些待沽的東西。

The focus of visitors to Shangri-la on Meili Snow Mountain is the unifier and divider between the tourists, photographers and the pilgrims. For most people, the highlight of their journey to Shangri-la is a view of this sacred mountain. It stands imposing and pure, jagged rock softened by a coat of the whitest snow. The mountain exerts a quiet power over his viewers, drawing them from near and far; people from different walks of life, of different cultures and faith come to set eyes on one of China's pearls. The mountain, for most tourists, is a background for a picture of themselves. Anyone can see the greatness and beauty of the landscape, but not everyone respects it and appreciates it. For many, it is not the mountain they come to see. What they want is to put themselves in that beautiful landscape, associate themselves with it, and transfer some of its beauty and purity to themselves. We are believers in presentation. If one takes an object, for instance, a shirt, and places that shirt in a stall at street market, and then takes an identical shirt and places it in the finest boutique, the price which customers would be willing to pay for the two shirts would be vastly different. Perhaps the shirt in the street stall sells for 40 yuan, whereas the shirt in the boutique sells for 180 yuan. The price and perceived value is entirely dependant on the surroundings. People sometimes are like objects for sale.

太子廟　老僧人

現代生活已經變成一系列的包裝。我們用財產、頭銜、聲望來包裝自己。我們購買的任何東西都是經過包裝的。我們購買一個產品，經常是購買好看的包裝而非產品。包裝付出的價格高於產品本身。這就是包裝本來希望達到的形象，表明這就是顧客真正希望購買的東西。事實上，許多人也用同樣的方法看待人事物，根據他們的環境做判斷。有的人喜歡由刻意挑選過的人包圍著自己，使自己顯得更有價值，甚至驕傲炫耀自己和名人合影的照片。人們喜歡從其他人身上獲取自身的價值，所以，有些人希望從美麗的自然風光中得到價值並不奇怪。他們不在乎自己的內涵，而從外界尋找美麗，再把自己安置其中，然後拍攝下來。把這些照片放到相簿裡面，再驕傲地拿給別人看。這是捕捉到底片上的生活，是否抓到了自己的內心呢？生活是否如同照片般愉悅呢？

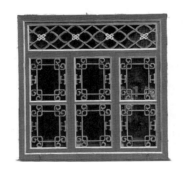

Modern life has become a series of packaging. We package ourselves with possessions, titles, and prestigious company. Everything we buy is packaged, and often we purchase for the packaging rather than the actual product. It is the image that the package projects, the promises that it makes that we are really buying into. People also look at other people the same as they look at packaged items, judging them by their surroundings. The people that individuals surround themselves with are sometimes there only to make themselves look better. So many people proudly display photos of themselves next to some famous public figure. People like to gain value from other people, and so, it is only natural that people also like to gain value from beautiful natural settings. The beauty within themselves is not enough, and so they come to find beauty in the exterior world within which they can place themselves. Then they capture it all on film. Picture after picture of themselves. People fill albums with such photos and display them proudly. It is a life captured on film, but is it captured in their hearts? Is it all as enjoyable as the pictures make it seem?

在梅里雪山前。　李玉祥／攝

關係 · 攝影師

　　攝影師就不同了。他們不將自己放到照片裡，而是盡力拍攝梅里雪山的美麗。他們了解山的美麗和山打動人的力量。他們要求自己捕捉雪山最輝煌的一刻。許多人激動地在黎明前醒來，在第一道陽光照射在雪山前佔據理想的拍攝位置。梅里雪山經常包裹在雲層裡，令攝影師倍感失望。只好第二天來，第三天再來。每個凌晨都包含攝影師的期望，他們恨不得禱告上蒼，企求雪山顯露崢嶸。很多人等待幾個星期，就是為了拍攝已經被無數人拍攝了無數次的雪山。在他們旁邊還有許多人在拍攝相同的照片。這是一種奇特的崇拜形式。結果如何了呢？也許他們拍攝到最理想的雪山，也許在書和雜誌裡可以看到他們拍的梅里雪山，使得他們為自己的拍攝技術感到驕傲。但是我認為去這麼遠的地方只是為了表現拍攝技術實在太奢侈了。他們好像以為佔有一張美麗的梅里雪山的照片，就是在某種程度上佔有或征服雪山。人都是有征服偉大事物的欲望，那麼他們當然不會漏掉偉大的梅里雪山。

　　Photographers are different. They do not put themselves in the photograph, but instead, strive to take the perfect photo of Meili Snow Mountain. They understand the beauty of the mountain and the power it has to move people. In order to capture the mountain at its most beautiful moment, many wake well before dawn and rush to set their camera in the ideal location before the first light of day breaks over the mountains. Meili is often shrouded in a cloak of clouds, disappointing the anxious photographers. And so they come the next day, and the next, lining up every morning with all the other photographers, all hoping, maybe even praying, for the mountain to reveal itself. Some wait for weeks, all for a photograph of a mountain that has been photographed countless times by others, and that is being photographed at the same time by the people beside them. It is a strange form of worship. What is the meaning in the end? That one can hold in their hand, maybe even see published in a book or magazine, the photo that they took of Meili? To have that, they can feel proud of their own skill. But, I think that it goes beyond the mere exhibition of ability. It seems to me that, for many, possessing a beautiful photograph of Meili is akin to possessing or conquering the mountain in some way. Man has an obsession with conquering all things that are great, and Meili has certainly not been exempt from these desires.

最希望佔有梅里雪山的人就是登山愛好者。在世界上自然條件最惡劣的地區，登山者最大的目標就是得到征服最高峰的美譽，梅里雪山是其中一個目標。儘管本地藏民強烈地抗議，認爲攀登梅里雪山如同入侵他們的佛主和聖地，但登山者仍然爲了私利而我行我素。第一次試圖攀登梅里雪山的人是在1902年，一個英國探險隊試圖攻頂，但失敗了。中國、美國和日本陸續有人前來。最後一次攀登是1991年由中國和日本組成的聯合登山隊，結果所有的隊員都葬身雪山。梅里雪山可不會輕易地屈服於人類的欲望。

The clearest attempts at possession of Meili have come from climbers. As in all the world's most extreme natural areas, climbers claim titles for ascending to the top of the highest peaks and Meili has been the aim of several attempts. Despite protests from local Tibetan people who saw these climbs as an assault on their god and holy grounds, the climbers continue with their egocentric missions. A climb of the mountain was first attempted in 1902 by a group of British explorers and failed. Other groups from China, the United States and Japan also attempted. The last attempt in 1991 was by a team of Chinese and Japanese. Meili does not give in to man's desires so easily, and these last climbers all perished on his peak.

明永恰冰川下　轉山者

在很多方面，攝影師和攀登者差不多。他們佔有一個目標的方法不是直接、物理性的，但目的相同，只不過是另一種形式。攝影師透過自己的鏡頭觀察外界，他們試圖捕捉各種畫面。攝影師捕捉的事物，無論是人、地方或物體，都具有一定的美感。在梅里雪山這個主題上，攝影師希望得到比美更多的東西。爲什麼有這麼多的人迷戀雪山，爲了雪山的一瞬花費這麼多時間？這是因爲雪山具有某種吸引人們到此的力量，值得他們等待，激勵他們祈禱完美的光線，而這種力量同樣吸引著遊客和朝聖者。這種力量可以產生神話、寓言和歌謠。梅里雪山有一種讓人渴望得到的難以置信的力量。光目睹是不夠的，他們試圖佔有。於是，人們賦予自己一個不可能完成的使命。

Photographers, in many ways, are similar to climbers. Their method of possessing an object is not so direct and physical, but the intention is still the same, it just takes another form. Every time a photographer looks through his lens, he is trying to capture something. Most often, that thing is beauty reflected in a person, place, or an object. In the case of Meili Snow Mountain, it is much more than beauty that is sought; otherwise, why would so many people pursue the mountain the way they do, spending much time for a few moments of opportunity. The mountain holds a power that draws them there, that makes them wait, stirring them to pray for the perfect light, a power that draws tourists and worshippers, that inspires myths, fables and songs. It is this incredible power that they hope to capture. It is not enough to witness it; they want to possess it. And so they set out on an impossible mission.

在攝影師的鏡頭前

扮鬼臉

人類永遠不可能佔有梅里雪山這樣的山。它的形象表現出一種無與倫比的美。但美僅是梅里雪山擁有的一小部分，人類在它的面前顯得渺小和微不足道。人們只有站在山下，才能感覺和讚歎它的巨大。雪山遠遠高出於世俗世界，人類的激情風暴無法撼動它。當我們安靜地凝視著其鋸齒狀的形狀時，可以感覺到它不屈不撓的本性。它是那樣的純潔和堅實，和人類的渾濁、軟弱形成鮮明的對比。遊客來了又走了，照片拍了一張又一張，很久以後，當照片上的色彩逐漸褪去時，梅里雪山依然存在。山屹立著，永遠存在，但人和有關人的一切卻如此短暫。人不能佔有永恆，攝影師拿在手裡的照片也只是山脈所有偉大特徵的一個影子。

No man can ever possess a mountain such as Meili. Images can be made that reflect an undeniable beauty, but beauty is only a small part of what Meili holds. Man stands miniscule and insignificant next to the mountain. The immensity of the mountain can only be appreciated while standing under it. The mountain rises far above worldly concerns and remains unshaken by the winds of emotion. Its unyielding and continuous nature can only be recognized while quietly contemplating its jagged structure. It is something so pure and solid that it stands in contrast to all the impurities and weaknesses of humankind. Tourists come and tourists go, photos are taken, and long after the colour has faded from them, the mountain will remain. The mountain stands still and has permanence, but man and everything about him is transient. Man cannot possess permanence. The photo that the photographer holds in his hand is merely a shadow of all the great things that the mountain is.

梅里雪山

朝聖者

🧘 關係 · 朝聖者

今年來朝拜梅里雪山的藏民非常瞭解人的短暫性。他們來自各地，甚至要在險峻的山區步行數百英里，每一步都五體投地對著雪山頂禮膜拜。他們這樣就是為了一座山。這座山對於他們已經不是山，而是主。他們來禱告佛主，心甘情願為它貢獻一切，包括犧牲生命。他們以它為中心不停地轉山。他們並不是來捕捉、征服它，或是獲取它的美。對於藏民來說，梅里雪山不只是美；雪山是神聖的，他們來此不是想從中取得什麼。他們把自己獻給了山。他們踏上艱難險途是相信有比覆蓋著白雪的巨大巍峨岩石更加偉大的東西。他們堅信有比物質世界更加偉大、比他們自己更加偉大、比他們一生所知道的一切都更加偉大的某種東西值得崇拜。

The Tibetan pilgrims who this year come to worship Meili Snow Mountain understand best the impermanence of man. They come from many places, some walking hundreds of miles over rough terrain, the truly devoted kow-towing at each step. They come because of a mountain, but this mountain is not just a mountain to them - it is a god. They come to worship this god and they are willing to sacrifice anything, including life, for it. They walk a great circle with the mountain always at the centre. They do not come to capture or conquer it, or for its beauty, for it is more than beautiful to them; it is sacred. Nor do they come to take something from it. They offer themselves to it. They make this journey out of belief in something far greater than massive rock structures covered by snow. They come because they believe in something far greater than the physical world; greater than themselves and greater than anything they will understand in their lifetime.

東竹林寺　僧侶們

中甸　藏族婦女

人和這座山相互給予和索取的關係，決定了朝聖者和那些欣賞美的人之間的不同。朝聖者來此是抱著對山和在其中的佛主的崇拜，他們留下他們的禱告、金錢和祭品。一路的旅途除了得到靈感和信念外，別無所求。而一般的遊客來到此地，卻留下沿途拋棄的垃圾，他們來此只爲索取照片和紀念品。朝聖者前來向山奉獻自己，從旅途中獲得一切，從自己忘我的奉獻行爲中得到領悟，而非要從山上獲得什麼。反觀遊客，只爲看到美麗的風光，逃避普通的生活。

The give-take relationship between people and the mountain defines the difference between worshippers and those who recognize only a desirable beauty. The pilgrims come to pay respects to the mountain and the gods within it, leaving behind them their prayers, money and valuable objects as offerings. They take nothing aside from the inspiration and faith gained from their journey. Average tourists come and leave behind trash strewn along their path and take with them photos and souvenirs. The pilgrims come to offer themselves to the mountain. Anything they gain comes, not from the mountain, but from their own act of devotion. The tourist comes in hopes of receiving beautiful views that offer escape from ordinary life.

居加村　祈禱者

　　人與山的不同關聯，源自於他們對生活的不同認知。生活在現代社會的人，希望改進自己外在的物質生活，生命的目的是試圖獲得更多的身外之物，並以此衡量自我價值。佛教徒花費生命的目的，則是希望去掉這些身外之物，例如財產、頭銜。朝聖者只帶最基本的生活用品步行數百公里，目的是淨化內心。佛教徒的目標是要認識眞實的自我，完成基本、啓蒙的自然狀態。他們堅信任何事物都是短暫的，所以執著地追求物質是無意義的。和現代人相比，他們存在的價值是由他們的行動和信仰來衡量。他們追求的是精神財富。

松贊林寺僧侶

The differences in the relationship with the mountain come from the different goals that people set in their lives. For people living in modern society, the goal is to improve one's exterior livelihood. Life becomes an attempt to gather objects with which to surround ourselves and gauge our own worth. Buddhists spend their lives trying to strip away all the external layers that are added to a person in the form of possessions, relationships and titles. For the pilgrims who have walked hundreds of kilometres with only the most basic of items of survival, the goal is to improve their internal beings. The purpose of life for a devoted Buddhist is to realize their true selves and achieve fundamental, enlightened nature. They believe that everything is transient; therefore, clinging to objects is meaningless. In contrast to their modern counterparts, their worth as beings is measured by their actions and beliefs. It is a wealth of spirit that they seek.

藏式群落民居

衝擊

　　2003年10月，中旬。我背著相機在一個村莊漫步。蜿蜒的土道在村莊中延伸。村裡的狗吠著向我撲來，繫在它們脖子上的繩索伸展又收縮。偶爾，一扇色彩斑爛的木門開著，可以看到裡面的大院子養著豬和雞。老婦人坐在水泥地上，面前放著一大堆豬草。一雙蒼老、佈滿皺紋而又粗糙的手，拿著鍘刀一上一下地鍘豬草。看到我，她停下手中的工作，微笑地用藏語對我說了些話。我在她後面的陰影裡看到她的丈夫。他右手拿著一串長長的佛珠，身子僵硬，步履遲緩。

2003. October. Zhongdian. I walk about a village with my camera at my side. The dirt path winds up and down slopes between the walls of many homes. Dogs see my approach and begin to bark, straining against their chains. Occasionally, one of the colourful wooden doors is left open and I can peer into the large courtyards often inhabited by pigs and chickens. Inside one door, I spot a woman seated on a cement floor; in front of her is a mound of greens. Her arm flies up and down, her wrinkled hand holding a large knife that is chopping at the mound. She does not notice me until I am inside the door, and then she stops, smiles, and says something in Tibetan. Behind her, in the shadows, I see her husband. His right hand holds a long string of Buddhist beads and he walks forward with a stiff bearing.

居加村　長年的跪拜將地板磨得十分光滑

兩個女孩用普通話和我交談。交談時，老婦人繼續鍘豬草，她的丈夫則順著梯子慢慢爬到二樓。女孩興奮地要我也跟上去，還說了一些我聽不懂的話。我順著吱吱嘎嘎的梯子上去，樓上有一間房屋，門的另一側有一個很大的神龕。婦人的丈夫在屋裡，站在神龕前，輕聲低喃。然後，他拖著衰老的身軀爬倒在佈滿灰塵的樓板上。粗糙的臉頰緊貼著粗糙的木板，向前伸出雙手伏著地板。多年虔誠的禱告，使得雙手伏著的地板被磨擦得平滑光亮。後來，兩個女孩帶我出去，她們說這裡很貧窮，問我在美國的生活如何。這時，來了兩個小孩子圍著我們繞圈，歡笑喊叫。女孩和小孩子一同玩耍，詢問也在歡笑中結束。

中旬藏族小孩

Two young girls also appear and speak with me in Mandarin. As I talk with them, the old woman goes back to chopping and the old man starts to make his way slowly up a ladder to the second floor. The girls excitedly tell me to follow, saying something that I cannot quite understand. I climb up the creaky ladder to the second floor where a room is set aside. Beyond the doorway is a large shrine. The old man is inside, standing in front of the shrine, murmuring softly. Then, his aged body drops to the dull, dusty floor. The wrinkled skin of his forehead touches the rough wood, and his palms press out in front of him moving along two spots on the boards worn smooth by years of his devotion. Later, as they walk me away from their house, the two girls begin to tell me how poor they are. As they ask me about life in the States, two children run up and begin circling us, yelling and laughing. The girls begin to play with the children, and the question is lost in the waves of laughter.

這些封閉地區的開放，爲當地人帶來巨大的衝擊，他們不再以過去的眼光看待傳統的生活方式。現在，他們被遊客帶來的新鮮生活吸引，因爲很容易就可以比較二者的優劣。而遊客卻被居民的民歌、舞蹈、傳統慶典，甚至簡單而近乎原始的生活方式所吸引。遊客想在藏民面前掩飾兩個世界的不同已經不可能了。在地人無法對遊客帶來的大量財富視而不見。他們開始渴望得到過去從未感到需要的東西。很自然地，他們開始比較自己和遊客的物質生活，於是，逐漸產生不滿。當然，任何地區的人民都會經歷這種過程。如何認識現狀並以何種方式與世界發生聯繫，只是時間的問題。

With the opening of formerly untouched areas to tourism comes a crashing end to the local people's ability to go on seeing their way of life as if they saw it before. Suddenly, they are an attraction to others for some of the qualities their lives possess, and it is not difficult to conclude what those qualities are. Visitors are attracted to their songs, dances, traditional celebrations, but also to their simple and rather primitive way of life. Even if the visitor has only the best of intentions, it is nearly impossible to hide the fact that two different worlds are meeting. The local people are not blind to the wealth that many visitors carry on them, sometimes like cloaks of superiority. They see it and then they begin to desire things they have never felt the need for before. They naturally start to compare their material lives with those of the visitors and the feeling of dissatisfaction slowly begins to creep into their minds. This is of course a bridge that all people from these areas will eventually have to cross and it is only a matter of time before they are faced with the reality of the place they hold and how they relate to the rest of this world.

在藏族婚禮的慶典上，婦女們圍坐一桌

中甸 藏族婦女以她羞怯的目光承受著未知的來臨

現在是這樣的一個時代：源源不斷的新事物和不同價值標準充斥新世界。這些變化帶來許多問題。它促使人們努力地與固有觀念，包括過去認爲是滿意的生活方式做出協調。對他們來說，城鎮和農村的面貌短短幾年就發生很大的改變，使得他們沒有時間消化已經做出的跳躍。他們不斷承受新文明的壓力，努力使自己的頭露出水面而不被淹沒，並希望在這個日新月異的時代不要落後其他地方，而打開這個新時代大門的鑰匙是財富。

It is a period of time that brings many questions to the minds of people who try and reconcile the past and their original concept of what is a satisfactory lifestyle with the influx of the new world and its different standards. For these people, the changes come fast, the face of their towns and villages changing within a few years, and little time is given to come to grips with the leaps they are making. They are caught in pressing waves of change and strive to keep their heads above water and not to be drowned and left behind as the rest of the country rushes forward towards a new age whose key is financial wealth.

金錢與幸福

在中甸和德欽，我所到之處，人們都在訴說自己的貧窮。這些人生活在寬敞的住宅裡，有著牢固的家庭關係，享用新鮮的食物，有自己的廟宇和自由信仰的宗教，生活在世界上最美麗的環境裡，呼吸新鮮的空氣，在清新的夜晚能看見佈滿繁星的廣闊夜空。在這個世界上，很少有人擁有這樣的生活，但是他們卻不認爲自己周邊的環境就是最大的物質財富。

婚禮

Everywhere I traveled in Zhongdian and Deqin, people claimed poverty. These are people who live in expansive homes, have strong family relationships, fresh food to eat, temples and the freedom to practice religion. They live within some of the world's most beautiful landscapes, breathe fresh air and, on a clear night, can see a vast sky full of stars. Few people in this world can claim the same. But this is a world that does not value these conditions as much as it values material wealth.

不幸的是，在這個世界上，很多人還是以財富的數量來衡量世界的進步。有人提出了財富和幸福成正比的理論，有多少金錢就有多少幸福。每個人都希望得到幸福，這種想法導致他們必須追逐萬能的金錢。金錢變成生存的理由，金錢可以解決所有問題，這種信念根深蒂固。有人說：「如果我有更多的金錢，我就不會爲帳單犯愁，我就可以生活在舒適的房屋裡，我就可以享受世界上最美味的食物，我就可以擁有人人羨慕的轎車，而且有更多朋友、女人和權利。」他們窮其一生追逐金錢，認爲這樣生活會更好，但卻忘了生活和享受人生。花費時間追求財富，卻犧牲了朋友之間最親密的關係。追求金錢需要謊言和欺騙，結果因此喪失本來擁有的誠實，變成貪婪而不知足的人。這種人以爲只要擁有龐大的財富，就能獲幸福快樂。

松贊林寺　轉經筒和祝福

Unfortunately, the concept of wealth, for people looking to make progress in the world, is measured primarily in numbers and quantity. At some point in time, someone came up with the idea that money is equivalent to happiness, and how happy one is, is directly related to the number of things and amount of money to which one lay claim. Of course everyone wants happiness and so they set out in pursuit of the almighty dollar. Money becomes the reason for existence and the belief that money can make all problems go away is held onto tightly. We think, "If I had more money, then I wouldn't have to worry about my bills, I could live in a larger, more comfortable house, I could eat all the good things of the world, I could drive a car that would demand respect, and I would have more friends, more women. I would have more power." We spend our lives earning money so that in the future we will have better lives, but in the meantime, we forget to live and enjoy life. We spend our time in pursuit of wealth, sacrificing our close relationships, lying and cheating, sacrificing our own integrity, and becoming infected with an insatiable hunger for more, all the while thinking that once we have more, we will be happy.

尋找幸福時，頭腦中應該要具備某種程度的自由觀念。不只是外在財富，能否充分發揮潛能，能否從生活小事中得到快樂，都是自由的重要表現。如果沒有更多金錢、權利的需求，那麼我們就可以從渴望獲得這一切的壓力和不恰當的需求中獲得解放。從簡單的事物中發現快樂，能夠讓人充分體驗生活的各面向。將自我當成完整的東西看待，我們不僅要對別人真實，也要對自己真實，這樣才會擁有比財富更多的價值。即使他人和周遭的環境會限制我們的自由，我們還是可以在腦海裡自由地創造幸福。為金錢放棄自由，等於是束縛自己。有個哲人說過：「金錢不能購買幸福。」

東竹林寺　僧侶

To find happiness requires a certain amount of freedom within our minds. The ability to be content, to enjoy the small things in life, and to accept our personal value outside of possessions are important pieces of that freedom. Without the perceived need for gaining more money, more possessions, more power, then we are released from the pressures of obtaining them and the feelings of inadequateness. Being able to find joy in simple occurrences allows us to experience more fully the many aspects of life. To be able to look at our selves as someone of integrity, who is true not only to others, but also to ourselves, has far more value than any possession. People and circumstances can restrict many of our freedoms in our outside lives, but only we can create the freedom within our own minds that leads to happiness. But, so many of us give up that freedom to enslave ourselves to money. It was a wise man who invented the saying, "Money can't buy happiness."

最幸福的人

　　旅行中，我發現一些幸福的人，他們是我遇過最貧窮的人。他們用簡單的方式看待生活，只追求簡單生活的基本需求。他們笑時，是眞正開懷大笑，沒有沾染社會的虛僞矯飾，也不爲任何私利。有人說，這些人沒有受過教育，不懂今天的世界是什麼樣子，除了自己的貧苦生活外，什麼也不知道，所以容易得到滿足。然而，我認爲使他們幸福的不是愚昧無知，而是簡單淳樸的生活。也許這不是他們的選擇，但在基本需求不用擔心的情況下，這樣的結果是生活容易得到滿足。

　　I have discovered in my travels that some of the happiest people that I have ever met have also been some of the poorest. They look at life in a simple manner and concern themselves primarily with those matters necessary for existence. When they laugh, they are truly laughing. They have not acquired social pretences and do not act for someone else's benefit. It can be said that these people are uneducated, that they don't understand the workings of today's world, that they know nothing better than the poor lives that they lead, and so, they can be ignorantly happy. But, I think the key to their happiness lies, not in the ignorance, but in the simplicity of their lives. Perhaps it was not a choice they made to live simple lives, but the inadvertent effect is the ability to be easily satisfied with life when all basic needs are met.

中甸　藏族老人

婚禮上的藏族男人

大部分的人都有相同的目標，就是希望改進生活，所以他們追求財富。但不可避免的是，賺的錢越多，引發的問題也越多，結果反而必須耗費更多時間應付更多瑣事，使得生活充滿變數。沒有人願意放棄舒適的生活去過苦日子，但有人還是可以既生活好，又不使生活變得複雜而疲於應付。只要明確掌握生存絕對的基本需要，以及生活需求，那麼就只需關心這些和我們有關的事情即可。關心我們認為重要的事物，這些重要的事物就會更突出。問題是我們分不清什麼是真正有價值的。這是每個人都需要認真思考的事情。社會、媒體、家庭和朋友都會告訴我們什麼是重要的，但最終只有我們自己能斷定什麼才是本質，什麼值得奉獻一生追求。

Most of us have a choice, and so in the attempt to improve our livelihood, we gather more possessions. But, the more we gather, the more with which we have to be concerned, the more time and energy we spend dealing with them and the more complicated everything becomes. Nobody would be willing to give up comfortable living for the life of the poor, but one can still live well and not unnecessarily complicate their lives. Once we can define what is absolutely essential to existence and what holds the deepest meaning for us in our lives, then we can concern ourselves with these things. With our focus on only what is important, then these aspects can only grow stronger. The problem is that we become confused as to what we truly value. It is something that everyone needs to consider very carefully. Society, media, family and friends all tell us what is important, but, in the end, only ourselves can define what is essential to us, and what is worth devoting our lives to.

瑪尼堆上的經文

從中甸到尼西，公路旁散落的藏族村莊

神話與真實

在我看來，香格里拉這個詞帶有濃厚的神話意味。當我來到這個叫做香格里拉的地方時，它就是我尋找的神話。我看到粉紅色的亭閣在落日的餘暉中泛著微光，以及藍色月光照耀下的農村院落。我認為這是逃避現實生活的理想避難所，能使平時的生活成為遙遠的記憶。在這裡，世界事務只是自以為是的人玩弄的微不足道的遊戲，緊張的工作也會變成輕鬆的晚餐。這是一個到處都是公正和公平、人民享有平等機會的世界。人們和平相處，人與自然也和諧共存。在香格里拉，遊客目睹了烏托邦式的生活方式之後，頭腦就會慢慢地受到感化。這就是神話。

For me, the word Shangri-la is heavy with myth. When I came to the place named Shangri-la, it was the myth that I hoped to find. I had visions of pink pavilions shimmering in the afternoon sun and courtyards awash with the pale light of the blue moon. In my head, it was an escape from reality into a blissful haven that made the everyday world only a distant memory. Here, world matters would only be trivial games played by people who knew nothing better, and the most pressing issue would be what to have for dinner that evening. It would be a world where all was just and fair, and people were given equal opportunity. Peace would prevail between people and harmony would exist between man and nature. By just being in Shangri-la, gradual enlightenment would slowly flow into the minds of all visitors as they witnessed the utopian way of life. This was the myth.

帶著這種想法，尋找這樣的一個地方，幾乎不可能實現。如果有人來尋找《消失的地平線》一書所描繪的香格里拉形象，他永遠都找不到。這是試圖將幻想變成現實的無謂努力。滿懷希望的人當然會感到沮喪。也許有人會認為我批評有關香格里拉的想法太嚴厲。畢竟現在改名為香格里拉的中甸還是一個充滿泥土芬芳和世俗風景的真實之地。我的問題是 ——我正在將一個真實的地方和一個神話進行比較。真實從來不會像夢想那樣富於吸引力。我必須問自己，什麼是我的想法？我想把自己對香格里拉的尋找之路書寫下來。我在尋找香格里拉時，靈感激勵我，同時也使我失望，我已經談論過太多這類的事，但現在，我認為我們應該從不同的角度來看待這個問題。

With such notions, the possibility of finding such a place is limited to the point of being impossible. If one goes searching for Shangri-la with the images from Lost Horizon in mind, one will never find it. This is trying to locate fiction within reality. Naturally, one's hopes will be dashed at first sight. Perhaps someone reading this will think that I have criticized the idea of Shangri-la too harshly. After all, Zhongdian, now named Shangrila, is a real place, with all the dirt and mundane aspects of reality. Here rests my problem- I am comparing an actual place to a myth. Of course the reality can never live up to the fantasy. So, I have to ask myself, what is my point here? I said at the beginning of this writing that I would be talking about my experiences with, and my own search for, Shangri-la. I have talked much about the things that have inspired me and disappointed me in that search. But, now, I think that it is time to look at things from a different angle

中甸　負重者

朝聖者的微笑

天堂的滋味

　　對於每個人而言,人間天堂都有一個獨特的形狀,由他們自己的理想和經驗構成,而這不是他人能夠傳授的。人間天堂存在於我們希望擁有的物質和特性之中,但卻不會出現在生活中。在這些虛幻中,我們架構了美好的生活藍圖,然而,即使實現了某些夢想,這些實現了的夢想也永遠不會像想像中的完美。每個人的認知有所不同,這種不同包括出生背景和文化差異等因素造成的。當人們在自己生命的旅程中遊歷時,為了財富、知識、幸福、愛情、靈感、讚美等,必須進行各種探索。完成這些事情會帶來滿足感,以及享受生活和事業的成功所帶來的成就感。如果人間天堂存在,這就意味著我們為日常生活、志向抱負、艱苦工作、目標等而努力奮鬥的一切都喪失意義,因為在這個完美的地方,不需要努

居加村　男人

力,不需要雄心大志,想要的東西都很容易得到,一切都跟想像中的一樣。我們的技能失去存在的意義,生活失去方向,不再有值得奮鬥的事。

　　For everyone, paradise has a unique shape, constructed from his or her own ideas and experience, and is not something that someone else can hand to us. Paradise is found in those objects and qualities which we hope to have, but do not possess in our lives. From these lacks, we construct our concept of the perfect life. The fallacy is that our minds have the tendency to romanticize and even if we do achieve any of the things that once belonged to our ideal dream, they never live up to the image we had in our heads. We all need meaning in our lives. What brings this meaning differs from person to person and is based on many factors including background and culture. As people move through life, many search for economic success, knowledge, happiness, love, inspiration, recognition, and so on. To find these things brings us satisfaction and makes us feel as if we have accomplished something in our lives, giving ourselves worth. If paradise existed, then it would mean that the struggle of our everyday lives, our aspirations, hard work, goals, were all meaningless, for in a perfect place there would be no struggle, no need for ambition, for everything we wanted would be accessible and all situations would be as one wished them to be. The significance of our actions or accomplishments would be no more and life would lose its direction and progress for there would be nowhere else, no other situation better to strive for.

迷惘　中甸

　　如果人間天堂存在，那麼我們不只失去生活意義，還失去酸甜苦辣的體驗。在一個完美的地方，幸福不再有意義。有快樂，就有悲哀；有白天，就有夜晚；有和平，就有戰爭。如果人間天堂沒有痛苦，那麼對於從未經歷過悲傷的人來說，他又如何知道這就是幸福？如果人們生活在寒冷和烏雲密布的地方，那麼他們一定渴望溫暖和陽光燦爛的日子。一旦每天都是晴天，他們的渴望就會消失。因此，我認為如果有人發現天堂，在那裡待了一段時間之後，那麼他很快就會覺得在天堂裡沒有什麼意義。

　　If paradise existed, then we would lose much more than meaning in our lives, for, in a perfect place, happiness would have no significance. To have joy, one must have sorrow. To have day, one must have night; to have peace, one must have war. If there is no pain in paradise, then how can one know they are happy if they have never experienced sadness? There must be balance. It is the people who live where there is cold weather and clouds who appreciate most a warm, sunny day, and the people who have sunshine every day who appreciate it the least. I would think that if one would find paradise, after staying there a time, it would quickly become meaningless.

不過，如果有人靠近香格里拉不帶有發現天堂的意圖，那麼他將會發現意料之外的美妙事物。沒有期待，就不會失望。當我們靠近香格里拉時，就像是我們靠近一個能成為我們朋友的人。當我們知道一個人的不完美處，那麼站在更

農具和瓜果

高的角度看待這些缺點時，就會透過這些缺點發現存在於生命個體中真實的美麗。人格魅力，可以掩飾缺點。如果以這種方式看待香格里拉，接受它的短處，就能發現它的驚奇。

If one approaches the idea of Shangri-la without the intention of finding paradise, then one has a much better chance of finding something wonderful beyond expectations. Without expectations, one cannot be let down. We must approach Shangrila as we would approach someone we hope will become a friend. Once we realize all the imperfections of that person, then we can look beyond them to the true beauty that lies beyond. When a true friend is found, flaws become unnoticeable in the light of all their strengths. If we are to consider Shangri-la as a real place, then we must come to accept its shortcomings in order to discover its wonder.

松贊林寺附近的藏式建築。這個地方經常被稱作「小拉薩」

民俗第一村　年輕的僧侶給寺院牆上的雕飾上色

現在的香格里拉是官方命名的地方，不再是神話中的天堂，但是它仍然可以使我們重新創造夢想。希爾頓自己就是這樣。他從來沒有訪問過喜瑪拉雅山，大部分的時間都在好萊塢——這個編織夢幻的工廠。但是約瑟夫‧洛克（Joseph Rock）卻說人間確實有夢想中的天堂。希爾頓根據洛克的描述，創造了一個無數人日夜思念的地方。爲什麼我們不能做同樣的事呢？來到中甸時，我們正在訪問一個眞實的地方，而不是夢幻；它是我們經過挑選並融入個人想像的香格里拉。沒有先入爲主的想法，我們要在腦海裡面寫自己的《消失的地平線》，我們是這本書裡的主角，去尋訪一個未知的世界。只有這樣，現實才不會妨礙我們創造想像中的人間天堂。香格裡拉充滿潛在的奇跡，我們必須用自己的眼睛去發現。

Because Shangri-la is now an official place in China, one must approach it, not as the mythical paradise that is to be laid out before us, but as a place where dreams can be created. Hilton himself did just this. He never visited the Himalayas, but rather, spent most of his time in Hollywood, the world's center of fiction. But, he took real places, described in the work of Joseph Rock, and created a fantasy that captured the minds of countless people. Why should we not do the same? When we travel to Zhongdian, we are visiting a real place, not a fantasy; it is up to us to pick and choose what we want to include in our own version of Shangri-la. We cannot hold onto pre-conceived notions, but rather, need to approach it is as if we were writing our own edition of Lost Horizon in our minds, only that we are the main character discovering an undiscovered world. In this way, the reality does not stand in the way of the creation of our own dreams of paradise. Shangri-la is full of possible wonders, but one must have their eyes open to see them.

山腰上的藏族村子

不一樣的香格里拉

　　2004年1月，昆明。我在寄住的地方看自己寫的文章。我必須完成這篇，但是組織想法很困難。香格里拉的形象在我的腦海裡流動，首先成形的是我的童年，然後是《消失的地平線》這本書吸引我來到中甸和德欽。我在閱讀旅遊雜誌時，看到有關這個人間天堂到底在什麼地方的爭論。實際上在被稱為「大衛營」之前，美國總統休假的地方也是叫香格里拉，還有在珍珠港被日本擊沈的一艘美國戰艦的名字也是香格里拉。香格里拉就是這樣一個名字，對於不同的人就意味著不同的事，甚至連我自己的腦海裡也有香格里拉的形象，無法有統一的認識。我翻閱字典，找到的解釋如下：

　　「香格里拉」（Shangri-la）：一個田園牧歌式的人間世外桃源；

　　「世外桃源」（Paradise）：一個地方、一種狀態或一種環境，在這裡可以找到完美的幸福。

　　2004. January. Kunming. I sit in my apartment looking over what I have written. I need to finish this writing and am having trouble organizing my thoughts. Images of Shangri-la keep streaming through my mind - images from my childhood, passages from Lost Horizon, and moments in Zhongdian and Deqin. I have read travel journals, and debates over the paradise's location. I have found that the United States presidential retreat before being named Camp David was called Shangri-la, as was a U.S. battleship that was bombed by the Japanese at Pearl Harbour. Shangri-la is a name that has meant many different things to many different people. I feel my way among these many images, still unable to grasp Shangri-la. I turn to the dictionary and this is what I find:

　　SHANGRI-LA - an idyllic earthly paradise;

　　PARADISE - a place, situation or condition in which somebody finds perfect happiness.

藏族家庭　祭拜之地

從語言學權威的觀點看，世外桃源顯然就是香格里拉，完全是人們對幸福不同理解的觀念。人們如何才能幸福？如果問一百人這個問題，會有一百個不同的回答。如果我要找到自己的香格里拉，就必須以自己的幸福觀念為主，忽視其他人的意見，甚至是創造香格里拉的人的意見。香格里拉是希爾頓的人間天堂觀念，不是我的。我應該創造一個截然不同的香格里拉。什麼能使我快樂？為了回答這個問題，我開始回溯自己的經歷。

It is apparent that, from the standpoint of authorities on language, that paradise, and therefore, Shangri-la, is an entirely personal concept based on happiness. What makes people happy? If you ask one hundred people this question, you will get one hundred different answers. And so, if I am to find Shangri-la for myself, I must think about my own idea of happiness and disregard other people's views and perhaps even that of the creator of Shangrila. The Shangri-la Hilton wrote of was his personal notion of paradise, not mine. I would create something quite different. To answer the question of what makes me happy, I must examine my own experience.

回望。　高星／攝

回溯

　　我開始翻閱曾經拍攝的照片，審視照片上的人和地方。每張照片都代表一個時期的片斷，某些原因使我按下快門。一些景像浮現在眼前：一張臉的表情，顏色的交會或一個意想不到的時刻。這些都表達了我個人的審美觀念。照片不只是時間的記錄，也是靈感的記錄。我回憶過往的旅行，回想那些帶來寧靜的時刻。我看到一位伴隨著古老舞蹈的節奏，坐在火邊紡羊毛的女人；老和尚低聲誦經，這已經是他無數年來重複無數次的事情。記憶帶我重溫過去：我曾經感覺到火的溫暖和冷冽而清新的空氣；我看過清晨的曙光和夜晚的天空；我也看過平靜的海浪，靜寂之中卻孕育著喧囂的騷動。我回憶起為數不多的時刻，當我看進他們眼睛深處時，雖然彼此沉默不語，但卻讀懂目光所包含的意義。超越語言的交流有如超越理智的情感，也像超越心跳的生命和具體空間位置的香格里拉。這些照片帶來了短暫的快樂，它們將我帶入那些曾經經歷過的時刻。

中甸　紡紗　火塘旁的舞蹈

I begin to look through the many photos I have taken, examining the people and places within them. Each photo is a representation of a fraction of a moment that for some reason inspired me to press the shutter of my camera. Something in the composition of figures before me, the expression on a face, the meeting of colours, or the sudden opening of an unexpected moment, are connected with my personal aesthetic sense. The photos are not only a record of the moment, but of my inspiration. I go over my memories of my travels and come across those that leave me with a sense of tranquility. I remember the motion of the fingers of a woman who sat by a fire spinning wool, the steps of an ancient dance, and the whispered chanting of an old monk reciting prayers as he has done for countless years. My memory takes me to where I can feel the warmth of a fire and the crispness of fresh air, where I see early morning light and the night sky, and where I can hear deafening silence and the calm of crashing waves. I remember the few moments when I looked into someone's eyes and understood what they were saying without the need for any words. Communication goes beyond language as emotion goes beyond reason, like life goes beyond a heartbeat, and Shangri-la goes beyond a place. Just by looking at the pictures before me I can feel the bits of joy that I experienced the moment I stood at the site.

135

當我拿照片給朋友看時，他們通常會議論美麗的風景或人物的表情，卻從來沒有看到我想表達的東西。照片隱藏的記憶，其含意遠超過照片的主題。不過，無論是什麼題材，都記錄了生命中具有特殊意義的時刻。人們會拍攝對自己特別重要的事件。例如剛出生的嬰兒、生日聚會、同學、旅行、婚禮、葬禮等，都是一些激動人心的事件。雖然我拍攝許多地方和人，但攝影仍然不是我的工作，我只拍攝那些能夠感動我的時刻，而且要有靈感才行。有些照片也許拍得不完美，例如光線不足、失焦，不過，完美根本就不存在於實際的某個地方或者某個時刻，拍攝的地方也不一定完美，完美存在於感動我們的特定地方和特定時刻之中，這些感動是我們自身的一部分，讓我們更有人性。在感動的地方找到幸福，才是最重要的。我沒有感覺時，不會拍攝。

來自四川的朝聖女孩

If I show my photo- graphs to a friend, they may com- ment on the beauty of the landscape, or the expression on someone's face, but they will never see it the way I do. For me, behind the picture lays a memory; it is much more than a sub- ject within a composi- tion. No matter what the subject, it is a record of a moment of my life. Most moments of my life pass unrecorded, but the moments of which I have images are moments that held special mean- ing in some way. People take photos of events that are of special impor- tance to them. If you look at someone's photo album, you see photos of babies just born, birthday parties, school classes, travels, special friends, weddings, funerals — all events with emotions attached. Although I am continually taking photographs of many places and many peo- ple, photography has yet to become a job in the traditional sense for me and I only take photos of moments that move me. For me to photograph, I must be inspired. Perhaps the photograph that results from that moment of motivation is not perfect in terms of lighting, composition or focal point, but, perhaps, perfection lies, not in the actual place or moment, or the photograph produced from it, but in the quality of that place or moment that moves us to feel, that reaches the part of us that makes us human. This is most important, for this is where happiness can be found. When I stop feeling is when I stop taking photographs.

在哪兒人們可以找到完美

　　透過照片思考我的旅程時，我開始釐清可以感動我的事物。有了這層認識，我開始能夠體會香格里拉。香格里拉意味著一個世外桃源，世外桃源的是指完美的地方。在哪兒人們可以找到完美？在人的頭腦裡。柏拉圖以自己的方式看待世外桃源。他說：「恆定和完美的形式不是日常世界的一部分，日常世界是變化和不完美的。完美既不存在於時間，也不存在於空間。完美只能被智力所認識，而不能被感覺所感知。由於穩定性和完美性，完美具有比感覺可以認識到的普通事物更大的真實性。因此，真正的知識是形式的知識。」所以，我開始思考。

前往江蘇的火車上，似乎伴隨著另一個自我。　李玉祥／攝

After looking at all the many moments from my travels, I begin to see more clearly the things that motivate me. With these realizations, I can also begin to grasp Shangri-la. Shangri-la is meant to be a paradise, and the idea central to paradise is perfection. Where can one find perfection? In the mind. Perhaps Plato was speaking of paradise when he said, "unchanging and perfect forms cannot be part of the everyday world, which is changing and imperfect. Forms exist neither in space nor time. They can be known only by the intellect, not by the senses. Because of their stability and perfection, the forms have greater reality than ordinary objects observed by the senses. Thus, true knowledge is the knowledge of forms." And so, I begin with my mind.

東竹林寺　僧侶

靈感與香格里拉

　　我的香格里拉存在於靈感之中，而靈感存在於我的內心和頭腦中，不過它們來自外界，來自我接觸的人、我到過的地方、我所經歷的一切。靈感是生活的力量，使得今天的生活對於明天非常有價值。有了靈感，夢想成為可能。沒有靈感，就無法完成任何偉大的事業。沒有靈感就沒有創造和進步。我們可以選擇生活在休眠的狀態中，或是生活在一種富激情和靈感的狀態中。有的人滿足於沒有主見，這樣可以輕鬆地接受過去一直存在的狀態而不必改變，並用最少的努力來混日子。我們可以跟隨無數人走過的路走下去，這樣可以消除風險，減少責任。若生活是這麼過的，那麼一生就是許多這種日子的總和。

My Shangri-la exists within inspiration. Inspiration lies within my heart and mind but stems from the outside - from the people I meet, the places I see and the experiences I have. Inspiration is a life force that makes today worth living for tomorrow. With it, dreams become possible. Never was anything great ever accomplished without inspiration, for it drives creation and progress. We have a choice whether to live a dormant life, or an inspired life. We can be complacent, accepting things as they are, making only the smallest effort possible to get by. We can follow the path laid out before us by countless other people, therefore eliminating risk, and minimizing our own responsibility. A day can be something only to get through and a lifetime an accumulation of those days.

承恩寺　僧侶

太子廟　黑暗中的油燈

另外，我們可以選擇能夠激勵我們的事情進入生活。我們可以建立我們自己的標準和時間表，走自己的路，選擇最有希望的路。危險存在於未知之中，就是這樣才刺激。當我們思考已學到的知識並運用這些知識來確定下一步的計畫時，有靈感的生活會使思維更加活躍。靈感在我們的周圍。世界不是一張空白的紙，而是一幅動態的、不斷變化的圖畫，這幅圖畫需要利用各式各樣豐富的顏色來塗抹。這個色彩就是靈感。

虎跳峽　秋日的花朵

　　Or, we can choose to live according to what stimulates us. We can set our own standards and timetable, walk at our own pace and take the path that looks the most promising. The danger lies in the unknown, but with that danger comes excitement. With an inspired life, our minds are active as we contemplate what we have learned, and how we will use that knowledge to make our next step. Inspiration surrounds us if we know how to see it. The world is not a blank sheet of paper, but a dynamic and changing painting from which one can continuously gather various arrangements of colour.

中甸　納帕海

靈感存在於香格里拉。靈感存在於中甸和德欽，存在於你的經歷之中。中甸和德欽一直是我難於置信的靈感根源。在那裡，天空藍、太陽亮、空氣空透、夜星清澈。這是一個可以沉澱精神污濁並用空靈重新組建的地方。如果有一個清晰的頭腦，那麼你就可以發現普通生活裡很難找到的寧靜。我在中甸和德欽時，平靜的意識讓我用嶄新的眼光看待世界，我發現一片難以置信的色彩流溢的世界。狂舞著的紅、藍、黃等純粹的顏色鮮明而強烈。這些顏色不是畫布上沒有生命的線條，在中甸和德欽，顏色成為可以移動變化的有機體。這裡有冷峻、雄偉的山脈和幽雅青翠的峽谷。巨大的湖泊反射著廣闊的天空。這種環境會讓人安心地敞佯在它的懷抱中，將你從日常生活、過去和未來的壓力中釋放出來，促使你放肆地體驗現在。靈感不僅存在於優美的風景之中，也存在於人與人的交往之中。

Inspiration exists within Shangri-la. Inspiration is rooted in place and experience, and Zhongdian and Deqin have been incredible sources of inspiration for me. There, skies are bluer, the sun is brighter, the air is cleaner and the night sky is full of more stars. It is an environment that helps wash away the contamination of one's mind and spirit and replaces it with clarity. With a clear mind, it is possible to feel a tranquility that is so difficult to find in ordinary life. While I was in Zhongdian and Deqin, this sense of calm allowed me to look at the world with fresh eyes, and what I discovered was a land of incredible color. Reds, blues and yellows were splashed about with the intensity of pure pigment, but these colors were not lifeless strokes of paint on a canvas, but were moving, changing and living phenomena. The landscapes were immense, and surrounding and combining harsh, majestic mountains with gentle, lush valleys. Vast lakes reflected even a vaster sky. This environment demands one's full attention, and in absorbing you into its embrace, releases you from the pressures of ordinary life, from the past and the future, and allows you to fully experience the present. Inspiration is not only to be found in the grand landscape, but also in small interactions with people.

東竹林寺　僧侶

松贊林寺的下午

　　我在松贊林寺廟靜坐了一個下午，旁邊還有兩個僧人。我們很少交談，多數時候沉默不語，品味著酥油茶。他們很年輕，像他們這個年紀的小夥子多半充滿了火一般的激情，但他們卻行動緩慢，有一種篤定和平靜。他們看起來不慌不忙，沒有壓力，也沒有理由打亂他們的平靜。他們不像其他人那樣連珠炮似地向我提問，而是讓我說我想說的。他們給我的感覺是對我存在的一種默認，就像一個家庭接受其他家庭成員一樣。他們沒有在我們之間設置障礙，也沒有任何陌生的感覺。他們就像兩個年長的智者，與外在的環境和諧相融。他們像是反射在平靜湖面上的群山倒影。

　　In Songzanlin Temple, I sat for an afternoon with two monks. We spoke very little, and mostly remained quiet, sipping yak butter tea. They were young, at an age when most young men are full of fire, and yet, they moved slowly, with precision and calmness. They seemed to feel no rush, no pressure, and no reason to interrupt their serene way of being. They did not prod me with questions like so many others, but let me speak when I wished. The feeling they gave was of an acceptance of my presence, as a family accepts the presence of one of their own. They held no barriers between us, or any sense of unfamiliarity. They were young, yet held the aura of two old, wise men and fit so perfectly with the landscape outside. They were like massive, powerful mountains reflected in the calm of a lake.

松贊林寺　他們，陪我坐過了一個靜靜的下午

松贊林寺

諸如此類的經驗使我的意識
更加清醒，視野更加開闊，讓我
的思維能吸收更多東西。我希望
吸收外界所有的色彩和空靈，這
樣我就不會忘記我在這些時刻的
感受。當時我非常感動，想著如
果放棄那些成天打亂我的時間和
思緒的無足輕重的事情，那麼自
己的生活會變得簡單而更有意
義。香格里拉是我改善自己生
活道路的最大靈感之源。看
到這樣一個地方，意味著
我親身體驗了發現偉大事
情的滋味。這種偉大不
僅存在於外部的世
界，也存在於自我
之中。

朝聖者

Experiences like these inspire me to become more aware and to open my eyes wider, in order to let my mind absorb more. I wanted to take in all that color and clarity and preserve it for my future reference, so that I would not forget how I felt at those moments. I was moved to consider all the unimportant things that clutter my days and my mind and imagine how much more meaningful my life could be with a little more simplicity. Shangrila gave me the greatest inspiration of all - to improve my own way of life. After seeing such a place, it was as if my tongue were wetted with the taste of great things to be discovered, not only in the outside world, but also within my own self.

東竹林寺

動感的香格里拉

　　我的香格里拉存在於動態之中。我的靈感源泉是持續變化的，所以在我的生活中，活動是必須的，它可以促使靈感源源不斷地產生。生活就是旅行，我們能走多遠完全操之在己。我們可以在外界和思想的某地停留，或者選擇前進。當然，生活有很多目標，一個目標就是一次旅行的終結。如果你爬山只爲了到山頂看風景，也許就會忽略一步一步帶領你來到這裡的重要過程。如果你沒有到達山頂，難道爬山的所有努力和時間就都白費了嗎？這只是你的想法。其實到達山頂所看到的風景，與人們在爬山的過程中看到的壯觀景色相比，只是一個狹小的視野。只想到山頂看風景的人，錯過的是一連串美麗的聚積，這些都來自微小的事情，但是它們比最後的山頂風光更加燦爛。活動的價值比成就更大，活動意味著創造成就的可能性。只要我們處於活動之中，就存在著創造成就的可能。沒有活動，就不可能有成就。

My Shangrila exists within movement. My sources of inspiration are continually changing, and, therefore, movement is necessary in my life to keep that inspiration. Life is a journey, but how far we go is entirely up to us. We can remain stagnant in location and in mind, or we can choose to progress. Of course, there are many goals in life, but a goal is the end to a journey. If you climb a mountain only for the purpose of seeing the view from the top, you miss the importance of all the steps that lead you there. And what if you never reach the top? Then was all the time and effort a waste? Only if you let it be that way. It is the small sights that most people pass on by as they continually search for the grand scene. What they miss is that the accumulation of the beauty from all the minor events is often much more brilliant than the final peak. The value of action is much greater than the value of achievement, for it is action that makes achievement possible. As long as we are in motion, then potential exists. Without motion, there is no potential.

中甸　男孩

　　所謂的活動，包括遊歷新的地方、認識新
朋友和發現新的經驗，當然也包括學習和創造
的大腦活動。和人體一樣，頭腦也需要訓練。
藉由學習、思考和分析的活動，幫助自己理解
事物。頭腦不只用來接受資訊，也要努力理解
這些資訊。人們以儲存大量知識爲傲，但是如
何運用和消化這些知識，每個人的思考方式完
全不同。活動頭腦，意味著既能吸收資訊，同
時又能產生想法。

Movement includes seeing new places, meeting new people and finding new experiences, but
also includes movement within the mind, through
learning and creation. Like our bodies, our mind
also needs exercise. To learn, to think and to analyze
are to move oneself towards understanding. The
mind is not only something into which we can feed
information, but also something from which we can
pull understanding of that information. People
pride themselves on knowledge and how much they
have put into their brains, but to have understanding and one's own thoughts is something completely different. To truly move the mind is to be able to
both take in and to generate ideas.

藏族婚禮上　觀看

活動也存在於香格里拉。中甸主要是農業地區，居民的作息仰賴太陽的運動。太陽升起時，開始一天的生活。日落時，就結束工作回家。晚上，街道空無一人，大家早早就寢。生活按照大自然的迴圈進行，每個季節都帶給大地新的顏色，給予人們新的工作。這是城市裡已經消失的節奏。在城市，人們不分晝夜在室內打發時間，在人造光線下工作；到了夜晚，同樣的光線又會照亮城市。除了與穿戴的衣物有關之外，幾乎感受不到季節的遞嬗。我們遵循自己的日程表，而不是大自然的迴圈，而且還要不斷承受來自生活和工作的壓力。很多人無視於季節的變化。工作一成不變，每天面對灰色的水泥道路，與四季的風景形成鮮明的對比。

中甸　田地歸來

Movement exists within Shangri-la. Zhongdian is a primarily agricultural place where people still base their lives upon movement of the sun. As the sun rises, so do the people to begin their day. As the sun sets, people return home, and at night, the streets are empty, asleep. Life is based on nature's cycles, each season bringing new colors to the land and new tasks to the people. It is a rhythm that is lost in a city, where people spend the day inside, working under artificial light and the same light lights the night. Seasons are insignificant aside from determining what we wear for clothing. Our schedules follow, not nature's cycle, but the beat pounded out by man. Seasons bring minimum change - the workday is the same number of hours, the daily tasks remain the same, and the concrete streets outside always remain grey.

通往迪慶公路旁的村莊

在中甸，人們依照地球的運行生活，節奏是規律的，代代都是如此。季節的迴圈就是一天的迴圈，終其一生沒有改變。春天帶來大地復甦的新鮮氣息，清晨破曉的光芒孕育著新生命的開始。夏天充滿生機，莊稼茁壯成長，正午的太陽熱烈燃燒，就像火熱激情的青春期。秋天是收穫的季節，夕陽金碧輝煌，是人的一生中鼎盛的時期，多年來的努力，都在這時有了成果。最後，冬天來了，舉目蒼茫，生意枯竭，彷彿行將就木的老人，徒留無盡的長眠。

自然的節奏

In Zhongdian, the people live according to the movement of the earth, a rhythm that is timeless, the same rhythm their parents followed, and their parents' parents, and so on. The cycle of seasons is the same cycle of a day, and of a lifetime. Spring comes with the fresh scent of renewal in the air, the morning with the pale light of the dawn of a new day and birth is the beginning of a new life. Summers are fully alive, the plants all having fully grown, the noon sun burns the hottest and adolescence is full of passion. Autumn brings the harvest of months of labor and fall color, the late afternoon light fills the sky with magnificence, and middle age brings the height of one's life, when one can begin to reap the benefits of years of effort. Then, winter settles in, bringing the world with it into a deep freeze, and the night brings the descending dark as old age slowly whittles away at life, bringing a person closer and closer, and finally into permanent sleep.

與雪山對話

　　當我仰望黎明中的梅里雪山時，陽光照耀在雪山的頂峰上，變化多端的色彩撼動人心。藍色，深紫色，流動的紅色，轉爲跳躍的橘色，然後褪成暖黃色，最後消失在潔白的雪色之中。梅里雪山彷彿在傾訴秘密，山頂的光芒變幻莫測，而這些光芒揭示山脈不同的特徵，就像我能夠專注於任何事物，同時又能從各種角度看待事物的各方面。環視一個物體，就可以看到它的所有特性。山告訴我，要我繼續自己的旅行，不要停留，在這個世界中不停地走動，可以發現生活中眞實的美，以及不同的文化、民族中都存在著的的美。山告訴我，生活要充實。

卡瓦格博峰山腳下的村莊

　　As I stood watching Meili Snow Mountain at dawn, I was transfixed by the changing color of light that fell on the sharpest point of the peak. Blue turned to a deep purple from which a fiery red bled forth and then paled to a vibrant orange that faded to warm yellow and then was lost in the pure white of the snow. It was as if the mountain spoke to me, saying that the light, by the change in its angle directed upon the peak, revealed the different attributes of the mountain, as I could focus my eyes upon any matter and change my perspective to see yet another aspect. By circling an object, I could see its full nature. It was telling me to continue my own journey, to not be still, but keep moving to discover the true beauty of life as seen from all over the world, through the many cultures, and from the many people who have something to teach me. The mountain told me to live life to the fullest.

瑪尼堆

創造與香格里拉

　　我的香格里拉存在於創造之中。大部分的人只會重複，很少人能做到創造。他們教授技術，展示技能，這些技能可以讓我們模仿前人做過的事，但只有在內心意識到這點，才能運用這些技術並創造新的東西。多數人將時間耗費在工作上，再造已生產過的產品，遵循別人的指導方針，容忍不屬於自己的標準。雖然創造新事物時，沒有人可以指導做法，但正因為我們的創造與眾不同，才獨一無二。從不同的角度來發現新的觀點，才是創造。什麼是有價值的？走相同的路，考慮相同的問題，說相同的事情，有價值嗎？如果是這樣，人就會變成一台只能做不同工作但缺少創造的機械裝置。創造是人的天賦之一，創造有助於進步。而靈感孕育創造，進步起源於創造。透過創造，我們為自己而活。真實的擁有，就是我們自己頭腦的擁有。

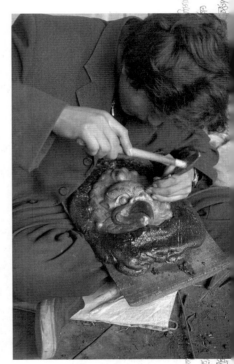

民俗第一村　鑄造神像

　　My Shangri-la exists within creation. There are many people who reproduce, but few who create. Others can teach us skills, show us every technique that will allow us to imitate what others have done before, but it is only from within ourselves that we find the ability to take those skills and create something new. Most of us will spend our lives working at a job that involves recreating a product that someone else has produced before, following guidelines set by other people and abiding by standards that are not our own. But, when we are creating, we are doing, not what someone else has instructed us to do, but what we have decided, separating ourselves from others by making ourselves unique. Creativity allows one to look at matters from different angles, and to find new viewpoints. What is the value of everyone walking the same road, thinking the same thoughts, and saying the same things? Man is then reduced to mere mechanisms, performing various tasks, but lacking the force that created those tasks. Creativity is one of man's highest virtues for only through creation can there be progress. Creation is fed by inspiration and progress by creation. Through creation, we live for ourselves, and truly own our own minds.

香格里拉存在著創造的可能性。香格里拉是和平與幸福生活的夢想。它像每一個夢想一樣，是我們頭腦裡的抽象概念。儘管這些夢想有時是純粹的白日夢，但夢想還是可以引導我們在真實的世界中發現一些希望的東西。每一個我們曾經擁有的、存在的，或者依然存在的希望，都可以是夢想。提到美好的生活時，我們的腦海裡會開始描繪著這種生活的細節、環境和快樂。這些個人的夢想給予我們一個直觀的印象，一個可以為之奮鬥的、具象的目標。然而，夢想不會總是夢想，藉由我們對夢想的具體化，有時會發現夢想是真實的。香格里拉就是一個例子。

The possibility for creation exists within Shangri-la. Shangri-la is a dream about the way life could be, about peace and happiness. Like every dream, it is something that is held in the abstraction of our minds. Although dreams sometimes exist as pure fantasy, dreams help us find our way in the real world. Every hope that we have ever held, was, or still is, a dream. When we imagine a better life, we picture in our minds the setting, the circumstance, and the joy. These are our personal dreams that give us a direction to look, something to strive for, and an ideal to try and give form to. But dreams do not always have to remain dreams; for they can often find truth through the way we embody them. Shangri-la is the perfect example.

藏族新郎和他的男儐相

瑪尼堆上的神像

對許多遊客而言，香格里拉是一系列計畫包裝的旅遊景點之一。這個景點被梅里雪山裝飾著，甚至有旅行社承諾可以到邊境冒險，去找尋詹姆斯‧希爾頓70年前描繪的世外桃源。旅遊路線早就訂好了，只要買票，那麼不需進行千辛萬苦的探險，世外桃源已經在等你。人一抵達，就被帶到預定的地點，吃糌粑和乳酪、喝酥油茶，觀看藏族舞蹈，拍攝梅里雪山的照片。對某些人來說，這樣已經足夠，香格里拉已經提供了一個普通生活所需要的娛樂。然而，跟隨預定的路線遊覽，根本無法與旅途融為一體，而只是接受光鮮亮麗的包裝。在這個包裝裡，有我們喜歡與不喜歡的東西。無論喜歡與否，只能被動地接受。很多人從未看到包裝之外，更加偉大的潛在事物。香格里拉是一個需要探索的地方，不是去發現，而是要在其中創造自己的旅程和體驗。

居家村　喝酥油茶

松賛林寺　準備酥油茶

For many travellers, Shangri-la is a packaged item to buy into. The package is decorated with images of Meili Snow Mountain, sold with the promise of a frontier adventure and the discovery of a paradise described seventy years ago by James Hilton. The itinerary is set, and all one must do is purchase the ticket. There is no need to exert oneself to strike out on a search; paradise is already waiting for you. One arrives, sees all the scenic spots, eats tsampa and yak cheese, drinks butter tea, watches Tibetan dances, takes a photo of Meili Snow Mountain and the package is complete. And, for some, this can be enough, for, already, Shangri-la has offered a diversion from ordinary life. But, in merely following the itinerary set out for us, we are creating nothing, putting nothing of ourselves into the journey, only accepting a glittery package. Inside, perhaps is something that we like, or maybe it is not exactly to our taste. That is the chance one takes in accepting it. What many people never see is that beyond the contents of the glittery package lie greater possibilities. Shangri-la is a place that needs to be explored, with people coming not to find, but to create their own journey and experience.

與香格里拉有關的最極端觀點是什麼呢？有人興高采烈時，是否也有人極度失望呢？我們可以在腦海裡毀滅或創造香格里拉，這取決於我們接近它的方式。香格里拉給了我們一個夢想可以實現的框架，但是它並不能因此使我們更容易得到理想中的世外桃源，而只是讓我們去創造自己的夢想。要親身體驗，不能走馬看花。實際觸摸鮮花，才能真正看到和理解這朵花。香格里拉不是一個輕易地將自己奉獻出來的地方，它不像一般的海灘旅遊勝地，不是只有簡單的沙灘、陽光、海水。中甸是一個具有多層次的歷史和神秘文化氛圍的綜合體，應該主動去理解這塊土地和土地上的人民，解開其中隱藏的奧妙。而我們，就和遊客一樣，要去創造香格里拉。我們希望從香格里拉得到的東西，有別於其他人的意義。我們已經擁有創造香格里拉的材料，現在需要運用它們來創造自己的獨特夢想。這麼做，賦予了香格里拉幾分真實性。

飛來寺

How is it that I have heard both extremes in people's opinion of Shangrila? Some people leave incredibly disappointed, while others elated? We can destroy, or create Shangri-la in our minds depending on how we approach it. Shangri-la gives us the setting from which a dream can be built, but it cannot hand us that dream. It is up to us to create the dream ourselves. We have to look and to experience. When riding one's horse to look at flowers, we need to get down off the horse, to touch, to smell the flowers, and then we really see and have some understanding of them.

Shangri-la is not a place that offers itself up easily. It is not like a beach resort, which is simple – beach, sun, and water – with no meaning beyond. Zhongdian is far more complex with layers of history and a mysterious culture. A willingness to involve oneself is needed to understand the land and its people, and to unlock its secrets. It is up to us, as visitors, to create Shangri-la. What we hope to gain from Shangri-la is something different for everyone. We have been handed the materials; we must figure out how to use them to make our own unique dream. By doing this, we give reality to Shangri-la.

居加村　身著華麗藏服的女孩

心中的日月

　　2004年2月，昆明。我在書店裡看書。書店的書架擺滿有關香格里拉的書籍
——《神秘的香格里拉》、《獨特的香格里拉》、《尋找天堂》等。然後，有一本
書吸引了我的注意，書名是《心中的日月》。據說，在中甸的藏語裡，「香格里
拉」的意思是「心中的日月」。平凡無奇的字句，卻包含豐富的含意。太陽代表
白天，月光代表夜晚，月光投射在大地上的光亮是陽光的反射。就像陰陽的黑
白一樣，太陽和月亮是對立的，卻又是不可分割的整體。它們的聯繫非常緊
密。太陽火熱，月亮冰冷，其吸引力控制著地球的大海。兩個天體代表一個完
整而親密的平衡。藏語的香格里拉告訴我們，「香格里拉」存在於我們內心的
平衡之中。這是幸福的規則。

　　2004. February. Kunming. I am looking through a shelf in a bookstore. The shelf
is full of books on Shangri-la - Mysterious Shangri-la, Picturesque Shangri-la,
Searching for Heaven. Then, one in particular catches my eye. The title is The Sun and
the Moon in the Heart. It is said that, in the language of Zhongdian's Tibetans, the
meaning of Shangri-la is "the sun and the moon in the heart." It is a simple statement
with incredible meaning. The sun is of the day; the moon of the night, and the light
that the moon casts down upon the earth is the reflected light of the sun. Like the black
and white of the yin-yang, the sun and moon are opposite, yet not separate entities.
Rather, they are closely connected. The sun is fire and heat while the moon is cold; it's
magnetic power controlling the earth's great bodies of water. The two celestial bodies
represent a complete and intimate balance. With this word, the Tibetans are telling us
that Shangri-la exists in balance within our own hearts. It is a formula for happiness.

松贊林寺中的轉經筒

太陽和月亮代表著運動、創造和靈感。當我們圍著太陽運動時，這個灼熱星球的光明和溫暖給予地球生命。人體的一部分得自於太陽，因為沒有太陽，我們就不能生存。當月亮圍繞著地球旋轉時，它扮演著靈感的源泉。有多少詩人寫下憂鬱的詩篇？又有多少戀人沐浴在月光之中，沈浸於默默無言的甜蜜？我們靈魂的一部分得自於月亮。讓太陽和月亮進入我們的心靈就，是維持著身體和思想的平衡，並讓平衡進入我們的生命。平衡可以解釋我們存在的各個方面，例如我們如何保持健康，如何區分工作和娛樂，以及如何與人交往。與朋友相交，只要保持給予和接受的平衡，那麼無論付出多少，都會覺得充實。「心中的日月」是一個簡單的概念，卻能產生有意識的努力。香格里拉是一種看待世界的方法及平衡生命的表現。它是一種自我心靈創造的態度。如果有人能抓住太陽和月亮所代表的所有意義，就可以找到心目中的香格里拉。香格里拉

德欽　白色的佛塔

無所不在，卻又不存在這個世界。正如在地球的每個角落，都能看到太陽和月亮。不過，在雲南的北部，也許能更輕易找到香格里拉，如同你站在高山上，就能更靠近天堂。

The sun and the moon are also representatives of motion, creation and inspiration. As we move about the sun, the light and warmth from this fiery star gives life to the earth. We owe part of our physical selves to the sun, for without it, we could not exist. As the moon rotates about the earth, it acts as a source for inspiration. How many poets have written melancholy poems and how many pairs of lovers have sat speaking of sweet nothings by the light of the night moon? It is to the moon that we owe part of our soul. To bring the sun and the moon into our hearts is to maintain equilibrium between our body and mind, and to bring balance into our lives. Balance can be applied to all aspects of our existence, such as how we maintain our health, how we divide work and play, and how we act in relationships with people. In giving and receiving affection, if there is true balance, no matter how much you give of yourself you will always be full. "The sun and the moon in the heart" is a simple concept, but one that takes conscious effort to maintain. Shangri-la is a way of seeing the world and a manifestation of a life lived in balance. It is an attitude that is created within our own minds. If one can grasp all that the sun and moon stand for, then they can find Shangri-la. It exists everywhere and nowhere. The sun and the moon can be seen from every place on earth. But, perhaps, in the north of Yunnan, Shangri-la is more present and easier to find, for as you stand high up in the mountains, you stand closer to heaven.

幻境

　　2004年2月，昆明。在最後一次進入香格里拉的前一夜，我做了一個夢。我騎著一匹馬飛快地穿過開闊的空地，當我們衝向遠方粉紅色的天空時，新鮮的空氣灌入我的鼻孔。在飛越這片乾燥的土地時，我和我的馬似乎成為一個個體。我們經過稀疏又鋒刃般狹長的草地，草已轉為模糊的綠色，看起來好像一條條綠色的條紋。這時，我身後傳來音樂，沉重的撞擊聲與馬蹄撞擊大地的聲音融為一體。我無法確定是否馬蹄產生了音樂，還是音樂成為推動我們前進的動力。當我抓住馬的脖子時，它那長長的鬃毛拂過我的臉頰。我不知道我們是在逃離某種未知的不幸，還是奔向一個極具吸引力的目的地，而且要在大門關閉前抵達。

　　2004. February. Kunming. My final entry. Last night I had a dream. I was riding a horse as he galloped through a wide, open space, fresh air rushing into my nostrils as we dashed towards a distant pink sky. My horse and I were one as we flew over the dry earth, the few blades of grass turning into green indistinct streaks as we passed over them. From somewhere in the back of my mind came music with a heavy, pounding beat that matched the pounding of my horse's hooves upon the earth. I could not tell if it was my horse's gallop that was driving the music, or if it was the music pushing us forward into an escalating momentum. As I gripped the horse's neck, the long hairs of his mane brushed at my face. It was unclear whether we were escaping from some unknown distress or rushing towards a magnificent destination that needed to be reached before its gates closed to us.

中甸　夢中的馬

慢慢地，低矮的綠色條紋逐漸增長，變成一片綠色的海洋，接著成為不斷膨脹的黃色深淵。高大的草叢掃過我的脛骨，刺得身體疼痛。太陽升起，陽光照在我的背上，一片溫暖。我們的影子投射到地上。影子就像阿拉伯童話中有魔力的地毯，我們在上面馳騁，同時把我們帶入天空，漂洋過海。這時，下方的黃色變得通紅，將我們吞噬進那劇烈而眩目的色彩之中。這些深淺不一的陰影，規律地跳動著，煥發出驚人的光輝，就像天空中即將沈落的火熱太陽。從馬的雙耳間遠眺，我看見遠方紫色的群山。我們移動得更快了，竭力追上拖在我們前方的長長影子。風在耳邊迴旋，寒意襲人。山變得越來越大，幾乎可以看見厚重的白色山峰聳立，伸進藍色的天空。但這些山很快就被我們拋在身後，我們在樹林中奔馳。樹一株比一株粗大，枝葉也越來越濃密，我幾乎看不清自己身處何地，只能憑感官來感受。

金黃色的玉米棒子

Slowly, the green streaks below us increased and turned into a sea of green and then to a deep yellow expanse. I began to feel the tall grass striking my shins, stinging them. The sun that rose above me warmed my back and cast our shadow onto the ground below us, like a magic carpet from an Arabic fairytale that we rode upon and would take us into the sky and sail us over the continents of the world. The yellow below turned to a red that swallowed us with its intensity, the different shades pulsating and glowing like the fiery sun as it sits low in the sky. I peered between my horse's ears, and began to make out the cool purple of mountains in the distance. We were moving faster, trying to keep up with our shadow that had grown long before us. The wind began to echo in my ears and brought a chill to my body. The mountains grew larger and larger until massive white peaks that jutted into the blue heavens surrounded us. But then they were behind us and we flew among trees whose trunks grew thicker and thicker, the canopy above us growing denser and denser until I was hardly seeing what we were passing, but more sensing it.

接著，馬停了下來。我們來到一片林中空地的邊緣，空地正中央是一個在月光下熠亮的池塘。我穿過這片白銀似的土地來到水的邊緣。彎下腰，在發亮的水面尋找黑暗。月光在漣漪上翩翩起舞，在這之下，我看到了自己。我看到了我的一生，從孩提時代到其後的許多年，我所到過的地方和經歷的事情，就像一部快轉的電影。我看著，直到看到自己在馬背上，穿過那些風景到達這片樹林和池塘。然後，我目不轉睛地看著倒影。水中，我身後那輪蒼白的月亮消失了，取而代之的是明亮的太陽。我醒了，微笑著。我找到了曾經失落的香格里拉。

在經幡的叢林中

And then my horse stopped. We were at the edge of a clearing, and at the centre of the open space was a little pool that glistened in the moonlight. I stepped down from my horse and walked across the silvery ground to the water's edge. Leaning over, I searched its dark depths with my eyes. The moon danced on the rippled surface and below. I could see myself. I was watching my life from the time I was very small, through all the years, all the places and situations I had passed, like a movie in fast forward. I kept watching, until I saw myself on the horse, rushing through the landscape and reaching the woods and the pool. And then, I was staring at my reflection. In the water, I saw that behind me the pale moon had disappeared and had been replaced by the bright sun. I woke up smiling. I had once again found my little Shangri-la.

大都會文化圖書目錄

●度小月系列

路邊攤賺大錢【搶錢篇】	280元	路邊攤賺大錢2【奇蹟篇】	280元
路邊攤賺大錢3【致富篇】	280元	路邊攤賺大錢4【飾品配件篇】	280元
路邊攤賺大錢5【清涼美食篇】	280元	路邊攤賺大錢6【異國美食篇】	280元
路邊攤賺大錢7【元氣早餐篇】	280元	路邊攤賺大錢8【養生進補篇】	280元
路邊攤賺大錢9【加盟篇】	280元	路邊攤賺大錢10【中部搶錢篇】	280元
路邊攤賺大錢11【賺翻篇】	280元		

●DIY系列

路邊攤美食DIY	220元	嚴選台灣小吃DIY	220元
路邊攤超人氣小吃DIY	220元	路邊攤紅不讓美食DIY	220元
路邊攤流行冰品DIY	220元		

●流行瘋系列

書名	價格	書名	價格
跟著偶像FUN韓假	260元	女人百分百—男人心中的最愛	180元
哈利波特魔法學院	160元	韓式愛美大作戰	240元
下一個偶像就是你	180元	芙蓉美人泡澡術	220元

●生活大師系列

遠離過敏—打造健康的居家環境	280元	這樣泡澡最健康—紓壓・排毒・瘦身三部曲	220元
兩岸用語快譯通	220元	台灣珍奇廟—發財開運祈福路	280元
魅力野溪溫泉大發見	260元	寵愛你的肌膚—從手工香皂開始	260元
舞動燭光—手工蠟燭的綺麗世界	280元	空間也需要好味道—打造天然相氛的68個妙招	260元
雞尾酒的微醺世界—調出你的私房Lounge Bar風情	250元		

●寵物當家系列

書名	價格	書名	價格
Smart養狗寶典	380元	Smart養貓寶典	380元
貓咪玩具魔法DIY—讓牠快樂起舞的55種方法	220元	愛犬造型魔法書—讓你的寶貝漂亮一下	260元
我的陽光・我的寶貝—寵物真情物語	220元	漂亮寶貝在你家—寵物流行精品DIY	220元
我家有隻麝香豬—養豬完全攻略	220元		

●心靈特區系列

書名	價格	書名	價格
每一片刻都是重生	220元	給大腦洗個澡	220元
成功方與圓—改變一生的處世智慧	220元	轉個彎路更寬	199元
課本上學不到的33條人生經驗	149元	絕對管用的38條職場致勝法則	149元
從窮人進化到富人的29條處事智慧	149元		

●人物誌系列

現代灰姑娘	199元	黛安娜傳	360元
船上的365天	360元	優雅與狂野—威廉王子	260元
走出城堡的王子	160元	殞逝的英格蘭玫瑰	260元
貝克漢與維多利亞—新皇族的真實人生	280元	幸運的孩子—布希王朝的真實故事	250元
瑪丹娜—流行天后的真實畫像	280元	紅塵歲月—三毛的生命戀歌	250元
風華再現—金庸傳	260元	俠骨柔情—古龍的今生今世	250元
她從海上來—張愛玲情愛傳奇	250元	從間諜到總統—普丁傳奇	250元
脫下斗蓬的哈利—丹尼爾・雷德克里夫	220元		

●都會健康館系列

書名	價格	書名	價格
秋養生—二十四節氣養生經	220元	春養生—二十四節氣養生經	220元
夏養生—二十四節氣養生經	220元	冬養生—二十四節氣養生經	220元

●SUCCESS系列			
七大狂銷戰略	220元	打造一整年的好業績─店面經營的72堂課	200元
超級記憶術─改變一生的學習方式	199元	管理的鋼盔 ─商戰存活與突圍的25個必勝錦囊	200元
搞什麼行銷 ─152個商戰關鍵報告	220元	精明人聰明人明白人 ─態度決定你的成敗	200元
人脈=錢脈 ─改變一生的人際關係經營術	180元	週一清晨的領導課	160元
搶救貧窮大作戰の48條絕對法則	220元	搜精·搜驚·搜金 ─從google的致富傳奇中,你學到了什麼?	199元
●CHOICE系列			
入侵鹿耳門	280元	蒲公英與我─聽我說說畫	220元
入侵鹿耳門(新版)	199元	舊時月色(上輯+下輯) 各	180元
● 禮物書系列			
印象花園 梵谷	160元	印象花園 莫內	160元
印象花園 高更	160元	印象花園 竇加	160元
印象花園 雷諾瓦	160元	印象花園 大衛	160元
印象花園 畢卡索	160元	印象花園 達文西	160元
印象花園 米開朗基羅	160元	印象花園 拉斐爾	160元
印象花園 林布蘭特	160元	印象花園 米勒	160元
絮語說相思 情有獨鍾	200元		
●FORTH系列			
印度流浪記─滌盡塵俗的心之旅	220元	胡同面孔─古都北京的人文旅行地圖	280元
尋訪失落的香格里拉	240元		
● 工商管理系列			
二十一世紀新工作浪潮	200元	化危機為轉機	200元
美術工作者設計生涯轉轉彎	200元	攝影工作者快門生涯轉轉彎	200元
企劃工作者動腦生涯轉轉彎	220元	電腦工作者滑鼠生涯轉轉彎	200元
打開視窗說亮話	200元	文字工作者撰錢生活轉轉彎	220元
挑戰極限	320元	30分鐘行動管理百科(九本盒裝套書)	799元
30分鐘教你自脑內革命	110元	30分鐘教你樹立優質形象	110元
30分鐘教你錢多事少離家近	110元	30分鐘教你創造自我價值	110元
30分鐘教你Smart解決難題	110元	30分鐘教你如何激勵部屬	110元
30分鐘教你掌握趨勢談判	110元	30分鐘教你如何快速致富	110元
30分鐘教你提昇溝通技巧	110元		180元
● 親子教養系列			
孩童完全自救寶盒(五書+五卡+四卷錄影帶)	3,490元(特價2,490元)		
孩童完全自救手冊─這時候你該怎麼辦(合訂本)	299元		
我家小孩愛看書─Happy學習easy go!	220元		

您可以採用下列簡便的訂購方式:
◎請向全國鄰近之各大書局或上大都會文化網站 www.metrobook.com.tw 選購。
◎劃撥訂購:請直接至郵局劃撥付款。
　帳號:14050529
　戶名:大都會文化事業有限公司
　　(請於劃撥單背面通訊欄註明欲購書名及數量)

尋訪失落的香格里拉

作　　者	金・羅絲貝莉（Kim roseberry）
發 行 人	林敬彬
主　　編	楊安瑜
責任編輯	施雅棠
封面設計	洸譜創意設計股份有限公司
出　　版	大旗出版社 行政院新聞局北市業字第89號
發　　行	大都會文化事業有限公司

110台北市信義區基隆路一段432號4樓之9

讀者服務專線：(02)27235216

讀者服務傳真：(02)27235220

電子郵件信箱：metro@ms21.hinet.net

網站：www.metrobook.com.tw

Metropolitan Culture Enterprise Co., Ltd.

4F-9, Double Hero Bldg., 432, Keelung Rd., Sec. 1,
Taipei 110, Taiwan

TEL:+886-2-2723-5216　FAX:+886-2-2723-5220

e-mail:metro@ms21.hinet.net

Website:www.metrobook.com.tw

郵政劃撥	14050529　大都會文化事業有限公司
出版日期	2005年10月初版第1刷
定　　價	240元
I S B N	957-8219-52-0
書　　號	Forth-003

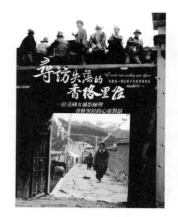

國家圖書館出版品預行編目資料

尋訪失落的香格里拉
／金・羅絲貝莉(Kim Roseberry)著
-- 初版. -- 臺北市：
大旗出版：大都會文化發行,2005[民94]
面；　公分
ISBN 957-8219-52-0(平裝)

1. 西藏 - 描述與遊記

676.66　　　　　　　94017352

大都會文化　大都會文化 METROPOLITAN CULTURE

尋訪失落的
香格里拉

大都會文化事業有限公司

讀　者　服　務　部　　　　收

110台北市基隆路一段432號4樓之9

寄回這張服務卡〔免貼郵票〕
您可以：
◎不定期收到最新出版訊息
◎參加各項回饋優惠活動